MEL BAY'S COMPLETE FLATPICKING GUITAR

by Steve Kaufman

CW00409766

CD CONTENTS

DVD CONTENTS

1 2 3 4 5 6 7 8 9 0

Visit us on the Web at www.melbay.com — E-mail us at email@melbay.com

Contents

Understanding the Notation and Tablature

Notes on the Strings 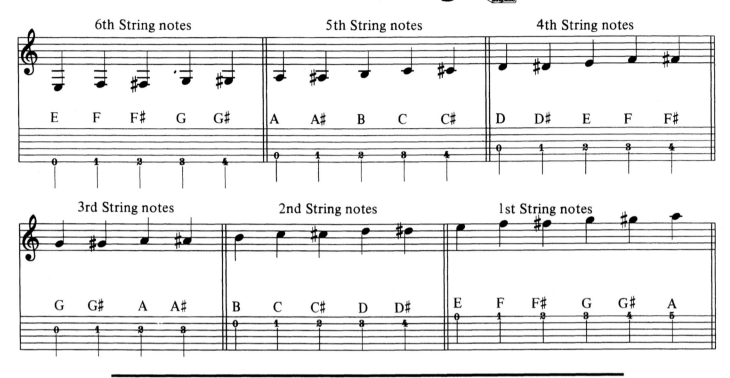 Track #1

Tablature is one of the fastest systems of learning to play songs that I know. You don't reap the benefits of reading notes, but it is a fast method of learning guitar material. If you don't read notes yet—learn how. You will be able to learn from any source once the notes are understood.

The tablature system is like a graph or a play-by-numbers method. The six horizontal lines represent the strings. The top horizontal line represents the first or high E string. The next line is the second or B string, and so on. The last line is the sixth or low E string.

The numbers on the lines represent the frets to be played. A zero ("0") on a line is an open string.

I've written enough notes to get started with this series, and you will pick up more information along your way through this course. Learn to read both the notes and the tablature. If you really want to learn the notes, it will come easily to you.

Types of Notes

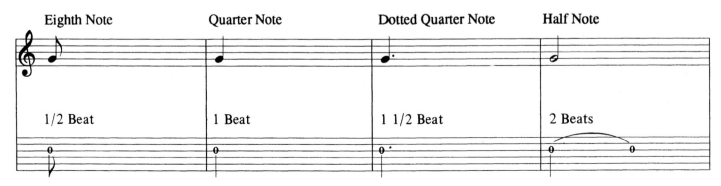

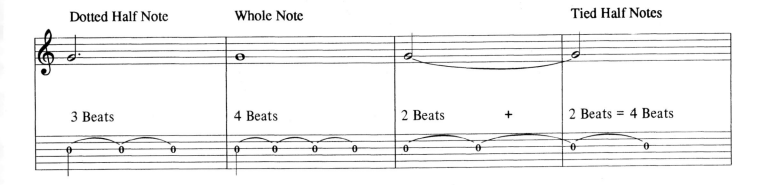

Dotted Half Note	Whole Note		Tied Half Notes
3 Beats	4 Beats	2 Beats +	2 Beats = 4 Beats

These notes are all G notes (third string open). They represent different lengths of time or different amounts of beats.

The first note is an **eighth note** (⅛). It is called an "eighth note" because it would take eight of these notes to make up a whole measure. A measure is bordered by two vertical lines. Look at the following exercise. It is made up of eight measures. Count the boxes that are made up of the vertical lines, and these are called the "measures." The eighth note will last half of a beat and, in my tab/note system, if there is only one eighth note, it is hit with an up swing going directly to the next note on a down swing.

The next note is a **quarter note** (¼). It gets a whole beat and is always hit with a down swing. Four quarter notes would fill up a whole measure.

Next is a quarter note with a dot after it, called a **"dotted quarter note."** A dot after a note adds half of the value of the note itself. The quarter note gets one beat—half of that would be half of a beat, so the dotted quarter note gets a total of one and a half (1½) beats. It is hit with a down swing. When a note like this is present, there is a 99% chance that you will find a single eighth note in the same measure.

The next note is a **half note.** It gets 2 beats. If there were four beats in a measure, the half note would take up half of that measure. The tab shows this note tied to another note. A half note also represents 2 beats when tied this way. Hit the note only once and hold it for another beat. It is hit with a down swing.

Next is the **dotted half note.** It lasts for 3 beats, and the tab shows it as a note tied to two others. Hit this note one time and hold it for 2 more beats to make a total of 3 beats. It is hit with a down swing.

The next note is a **whole note.** It lasts for 4 beats and is called a "whole note" because it takes all the time of a measure in 4/4 time—4 beats. The tab shows it as the first note tied to three others. Hit it only once and let it ring for 4 beats. It is hit with a down swing.

Next is a **half note tied to another half note** of the next measure. You must add the time (the number of beats) of the first note to the time of the second note. Adding it all together, this is the number of beats that the note should ring. If you had a dotted half note (3 beats) tied to a quarter note (1 beat), then the note should ring for 4 beats total time. It is hit with a down swing.

Play through the following exercise to get familiar with the notes and the tab. Be sure to watch out for the timing. All the notes are to be hit with a down swing. Play the exercise with the notes first, checking with the first chart to find where the notes are, then go through the exercise using the tab system. Play it backwards and forwards to help familiarize yourself with the notes and the tab. Be sure to play it backwards and forwards. Trust me—I have my reasons.

Play this exercise backwards and forwards:

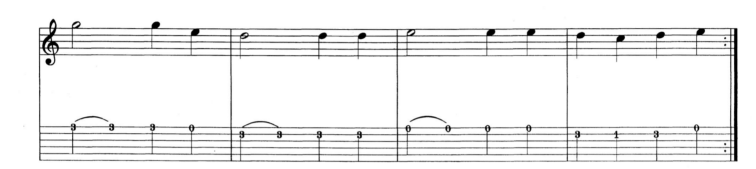

The next few examples deal with timing. The first measure shows four **quarter notes.** They are all hit with a down swing. On top of each measure is a row of numbers with a "+" between them. When you hit quarter notes or any notes larger than a single eighth note, they are hit on down swings and on the number. To see how this works, count out loud:

1 + 2 + 3 + 4 +

Now hit the notes when you say the numbers. Be sure to count steadily, and don't hit any note on a "+." This is the proper way to hit quarter notes.

The next measure shows **eighth notes.** It doesn't matter whether they are tied (or beamed) together at the bottom or the top, or whether they are grouped in sets of two or four. What matters is the right-hand motion with eighth notes. The first eighth note is always hit down, the second is hit up, and so on. Count "1 + 2 + 3 + 4 +," hitting the first note down on the number, the second note up on the "+," down on the number, up on the "+."

Keep it steady. There is very little time between eighth notes. They go as fast as you can count and sometimes faster. Tap your foot while you are counting. Notice that your foot goes down on the number and up on the "+." Your right hand moves the same way. Practice eighth notes while counting and tapping your foot.

The fourth measure illustrates **hammer-ons** and **pull-offs.** The hammer-on is marked by a slur or tie over or under the notes. The example shows an open string to the 2nd fret. Hit the open string and, without your right hand hitting the string again, shoot the second finger of your left hand onto the 2nd fret. You must shoot your second finger onto the string very sharply. It doesn't have to be fast—it just has to have a fast attack.

The pull-off is just the opposite. Put your second finger on the 2nd fret of the third string. Hit the third string and, without hitting the string again, pull your finger off the string. It is best to dig under the string a little so you will have a stronger, pluckier pull-off.

The next measure shows a series of eighth notes with hammer-ons and pull-offs. Pay close attention to the arrows and the timing. Be sure to count "1 + 2 + 3 + 4 +," etc., while you practice this exercise.

On either side of this measure are **repeat signs.** They are shown as two vertical lines with two dots. The repeat signs face each other. The first sign tells you that there is another repeat sign coming up soon and, when you get to it, go back to the first sign and play the section over again. In this exercise, play the measure for about two minutes without stopping, just to practice the hammers and pulls.

The next measure deals with **slides.** It is very important when doing a slide to maintain your finger pressure so that the note will ring the entire length of the slide and hopefully a little after the slide has ended. Slides usually involve two notes, as do hammer-ons and pull-offs—the starting point and the ending point. Your right hand hits them only once. Let your left hand do the rest.

Next we have **bends.** Place your third finger on the second string, 3rd fret. This is the note you are going to practice bending. Hit the second string and try to bend, or push the note, to the pitch of the next fret so that the 3rd fret sounds like the 4th fret.

It is difficult to bend the string and hold it for any length of time. The easiest way to bend a note is to put your third finger on the 3rd fret; your second finger on the same string, 2nd fret; and your first finger on the 1st fret, same string. Hit the second string, and push all three fingers up at the same time. Use the combined strength of all three fingers to achieve a smooth bend. Be sure to maintain the finger pressure, or else the note will die off before its time.

The last three measures deal with hammer-ons and slides in groups of eighth notes. By now you know the procedure; just be careful with the down-ups and the timing.

After you are proficient with these exercises, you will be ready to go through the course. Have fun and let me know if you have any trouble. Be sure to go through my advanced series after you finish this one.

Timing 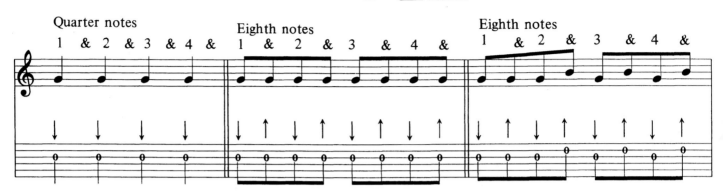 Track #2

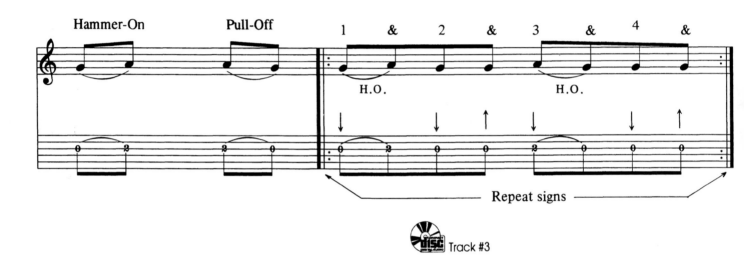

Repeat signs

Track #3

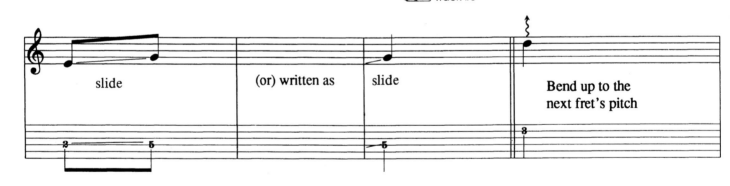

slide   (or) written as   slide   Bend up to the next fret's pitch

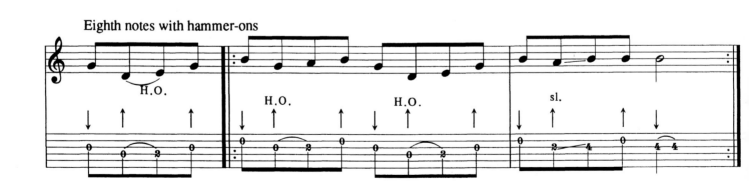

Eighth notes with hammer-ons

Let's Get Started

Tuning the Guitar the Conventional Way

There are several ways to tune a guitar. The most conventional method is to find a source of one correct note by means of a tuning fork or pitch pipe. You can get these at any music store. I use an E tuning fork at 329.6 vibrations per second. It has "329.6" stamped on the single pole end. This tone is equivalent to the first string open.

Hold the fork by the ball at the end. Strike the fork on your knee and push the ball against the top of the guitar. The whole body of the guitar will ring the tone of the tuning fork. Pluck the first string with your free hand, and tune the two tones together. You will hear a slight pulsation. This is the sound of two tones that are close but not perfectly alike.

Start to turn the tuning peg. If the pulse gets faster, you are turning the peg the wrong way. The slower the pulse, the closer you are. Turn the peg until the pulse is no longer audible. You have now tuned the first string to a standard concert pitch. Now you must tune the rest of the strings.

If you can't get a tuning fork or pitch pipe, you can still use the following method to tune the guitar to itself: Put your finger on the second string, 5th fret. This is an E note, and it should be the same as the first string open. Tune the second string up or down until the two notes disappear and sound like one note. Use the pulse test and listen for the waves. When these two strings are in tune, go to the third string, 4th fret.

This note is a B and should match the second string open. Get the second and third strings in tune, and go to the fourth string, 5th fret. This note is a G and should match the third string. Then go to the fifth string, 5th fret. This note is a D and should match the fourth string open. Next is the sixth string, 5th fret. This note is an A and should match the fifth string open. At this point, all the strings should be in tune. The strings will probably be out of tune if this

procedure took more than two minutes. Go through the whole process again to check everything and to fine tune the instrument.

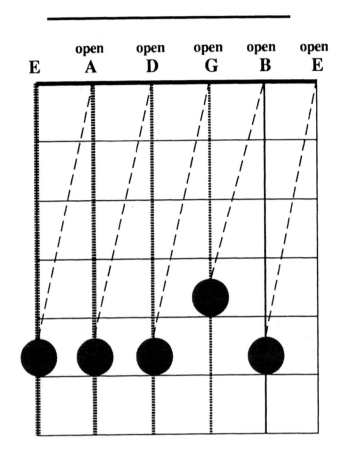

Conventional Tuning

The next thing to do is to check the intonation. This refers to playing a chord to see if it is in tune. Hold down and strum a D chord. If it isn't in tune, you will hear a string or two seem to jump out at you. Tune the strings that you think are out of tune and re-check the D chord. If a string/note seems to jump out at you or sound louder than all the others, then it is likely to be out of tune. Go through this same process with other chords, tweaking the string a little for one chord, then another. What you are actually doing is compensating each string to sound correct with several chords.

It takes a long time to tune using this method if you are trying it for the first time. It took me half an hour the first time. Now I have it down to about ten seconds. Like anything else, the more you do it, the faster you will become.

Harmonics

A **harmonic** is a sound that resembles a chime. When you produce a harmonic, you are dividing the string length a precise and equal amount between two points on the string. A harmonic at the 12th fret is an equal division of the distance between the nut and the saddle. Other harmonic points are the 4th, 5th, 7th, and 9th frets; but the easiest place to make a harmonic is at the 12th fret on any string.

Place the ball of your second left-hand finger over the 12th fret. If you are trying a harmonic for the first time, you will probably place your finger behind the 12th fret. To play a harmonic, you must be *directly over* the 12th fret (the actual fretwire). Don't push hard enough to bend the string. Hit the string and remove your finger. You should hear something similar to a chime or a bell. If you hear only a thud, then one or two things could have happened: You may have let your finger drift from directly over the 12th fretwire, or you may have been pushing on the string too hard. Try playing some harmonics on all of the strings at the 12th fret.

Tuning with Harmonics

The use of harmonics can be one of the most accurate methods of tuning. Be sure to have fairly fresh strings. Old, lifeless strings will give you an inaccurate response. Tune the first string with the tuning fork or pitch pipe. Play a harmonic on the sixth string, 5th fret. Remember to precisely place the ball of your fingertip over the 5th fretwire. This tone is an E and should match the first string open. Tune your first string until both tones are the same. You have now tuned the first and sixth strings.

Hit the same harmonic on the sixth string, 5th fret, and match it with the harmonic on the fifth string, 7th fret. Tune the two until they are the same. You will hear the oscillations more intensely using harmonics. Tune until the waves and pulses stop.

Now hit the harmonic on the fifth string, 5th fret, and match it with fourth string, 7th fret. Tune until the waves stop. Go to the fourth string, 5th fret, and match it with the third string, 7th fret. This is a B note and should match the second string open. Remember that you have already tuned the first and sixth strings? Double-check the harmonic tuning by chiming the second string, 5th fret, and matching it with the first string, 7th fret. If the first and second strings match, then all went well. If not, run through the process until everything matches.

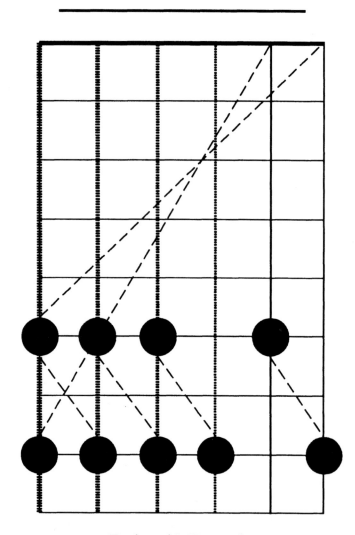

Tuning with Harmonics

Another double-checking method is to hit the harmonic on the sixth string, 4th fret. This note is a G♯ and should match the third string, 1st fret. The fifth string, 5th fret, is an A and should match the first string, 5th fret. The fourth string, 7th fret, is also an A and should match the first string, 5th fret.

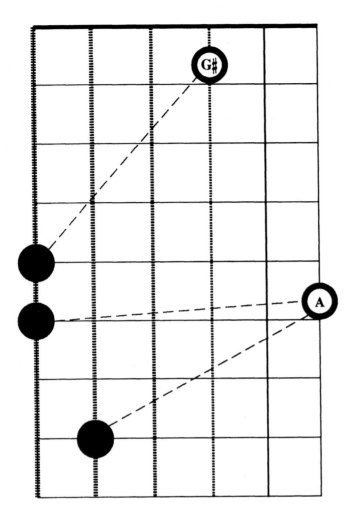

Double-Check Your Tuning with Harmonics

Tuning Your Guitar with a Tuner

If you have trouble hearing whether two strings are tuned correctly or can't hear the pulses and waves, then I would suggest investing in an electronic tuner. There are several types of tuners, all tailored to your specific needs and budget. They range in price from approximately $29.95 to $200.00. They all have built-in microphones. Some tuners have a jack on the side to plug an acoustic-electric guitar straight in, bypassing the microphone and therefore cutting down possible error from the microphone picking up outside noise.

There are basically two kinds of tuners—chromatic and non-chromatic. A non-chromatic tuner tunes only the six open strings on the guitar. With this type of tuner, you tune the strings by striking a string and watching a needle move from left (flat) to right (sharp). You want the needle to be straight up, centering on the bold line on the face of the tuner. Then move the switch to tune the next string, and so on.

With a chromatic tuner you can tune a string and, without moving a switch, move to the next string. You can also use a chromatic tuner for any instrument which is handy, making it economically justifiable if you play more than one instrument.

The chromatic tuner will tune all of the notes on the guitar. This is a handy feature that allows you to check the intonation of your guitar at different places on the fingerboard. These tuners usually have red L.E.D. lights that flicker and, in one way or another, show you if you are in tune. This is the type of tuner that I use because of its ease of use and speed. The one that I use retails for under $50. The more expensive tuners have more features: L.E.D. lights in combination with a V.U. needle-meter, metronomes, beeps, bells, and whistles.

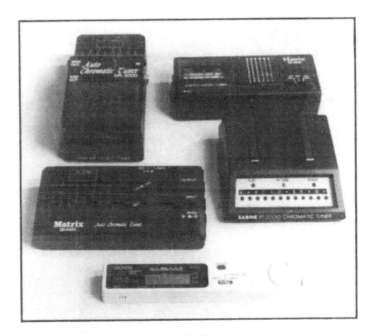

Electronic Tuners
Photo by Tim Everett
Equipment supplied by Murlin's Music World

Left-Hand Placement

The left-hand fingers should be loose, the wrist slightly bent, and the thumb should point almost completely straight up. You should be able to slide a pencil between your palm and the bottom of the guitar neck. I call this having "plenty of air" so your hand remains unrestricted. You do not want to hold the neck up with your left hand. The thumb and fingertips should be the only contact points. Remember that the more skin that touches the neck, the more friction.

Try holding down any fret with only the thumb touching the neck. Slide 7 or 8 frets, dragging your thumb along. Now try holding the same fret and gripping the neck as if you were holding a club, and try the same slide. You probably heard a squeak as you slid. This is the sound of friction, or too much surface area on the back of the neck. Too much surface area only slows you down.

Left-Hand Placement
Photo by Tim Everett

The Right Hand

The right hand is the source of 90% of your tone, speed, and articulation. I place my little finger on the pick guard. It is not frozen in place, but moves as my pick strokes move. The space between my pick and little finger stays relatively the same.

If playing in the bass zone (fourth, fifth, and sixth strings), the little finger touches the pick guard and pulls against the first string. This will give you a little more support and help you drive through the heavier strings. When playing on the treble strings (first, second, and third strings), stay about half an inch below the first string. Keep the palm off the bridge and the bridge pins. Almost all of the string vibration must pass through the saddle to the bridge, so be sure not to dampen or rest on the bridge.

Hold the pick with the first finger and thumb. Keep the second and third fingers loose. Don't make a fist. A contraction or tightening of the hand and arm muscles would be necessary to make a fist, resulting in too much tension in the hand and forearm. Stay loose. If you forearm gets too tight, wiggle your fingers while watching your arm and see which finger or fingers make the tight area of your arm move. Those are the fingers to concentrate on loosening up.

Angle the pick forward about 20 degrees for regular hoedowns, breakdowns, and straight-line melodies. Use approximately ⅛ to ¼ of an inch of pick for each strike, and stay even with the right-hand edge of the sound hole. For a clear, crisp crosspicking sound, move a little closer to the bridge and change the angle of the pick—parallel (level) to the strings with a tighter thumb.

Use a lot of follow-through when striking the strings. This will give you a sharper, snappier sound. Start your swing about half an inch from the target and swing about half an inch past it. You must also develop an in-out motion in order to miss striking the unwanted adjacent string. Six different motions will take place for each down-up swing—in-down-out, in-up-out. Over-exaggerate this motion in your practice. This is a practice technique to use when playing slowly.

Your stroke length will shorten the faster you play. This is normal. In order to play fast, you must minimize your motion. You will also trade volume when you gain speed, so be aware of this trade-off. Over-exaggerate the volume in practice, or it won't be there when you need it. Your volume switch is in your right thumb. The tighter your thumb, the sharper the attack and the louder the note.

Right-Hand Placement
Photo by Tim Everett

Correct Posture: Playing While Sitting or Standing

When practicing in the seated position, it is best to use a straight-back chair that has no arms—something like a kitchen chair. My favorite chair for practicing is an armless rocking chair. Sit on the forward edge of the chair with your back straight. Keep the bottom side of the guitar resting flat on your right leg. The back of the guitar should be about 90 degrees to the floor and almost against your body. Your arm should rest on the guitar with your elbow just past the forward edge of the box. This will allow your pick to reach the right edge of the sound hole and give you full down-up mobility in your forearm for strumming chords.

If you wear a strap while sitting, be sure to keep it tight. The reason for this is to keep the guitar in the same approximate position whether you are seated or standing. If you have ever seen Doc Watson perform, you may have noticed that, while sitting, his strap is tightened so that his guitar is about an inch off of his leg. Sitting or standing, the position of the guitar should feel the same.

Sitting with Guitar While in Seated Position
Photo by Tim Everett

Do not practice while sitting on a couch. Couches are usually too low and make you play in a semi-reclining position. The problem with this position is that it tilts the guitar backward a little and forces your right arm too far out in front of the instrument. This will lead to circulation problems in your arm, and you will soon notice that your fingers have fallen asleep. You have a large artery under your arm near the shoulder that can be cut off if your arm is resting on the edge of the guitar.

Standing while playing is very similar to sitting. There are two basic standing positions. The first position is keeping your legs about shoulder width apart with your weight distributed evenly between them. The second standing position is with one leg directly under your body and the other leg slightly bent and out in front. Put about 75% of your weight on your back leg and keep it straight. This leaves your front foot a little freer for tapping out the rhythm. I usually keep my left leg back with my right leg in front. It takes practice to play and stand. Try it a little every day until it becomes comfortable and your playing becomes accurate.

Standing Position with Microphone Placement
Legs are even, with one leg braced
Photo by Tim Everett

Understanding the Capo

The capo has gone through many changes since its inception decades ago. In the days of Flatt and Scruggs, a good capo was a No. 2 pencil and a strong rubber band. Now there are about a dozen different styles. All capos do the same thing. They raise the pitch of a song to a key that better suits the voice. If two people know the same song but have learned it in different keys, then the capo can transpose the song from one key to another.

Capos come in different shapes and for different budgets. The best capo is one that is easy and quick to put on and won't stretch your strings out of tune. Prices range from $3 to $60. The double-elastic capo was my first. It costs about $3 and is replaced every other year or so. Now I switch between several. The Schub capo seems to be the fastest and most accurate for me, while the Kyser capo works best for others. I also use a low-profile stainless-steel capo with bull horn as the contact point across the strings. It works very well but takes a little longer to get into place. You just have to try them all.

To understand the capo, you must first memorize this little theory lesson: **The notes start at A and go all the way to G and then start over at A again**—read this until it is memorized. A-B-C-D-E-F-G—A-B-C-D-E-F-G—A-B-C-D-E-F-G—A . . . and it goes on forever.

The next thing to memorize is this: **B goes right to C, and E goes right to F.** You have sharps (♯) between all the other notes, except B goes right to C, and E goes right to F. **There is no B♯, and there is no E♯:** A-A♯-B-C-C♯-D-D♯-E-F-F♯-G-G♯—A-A♯-B-C-C♯-D-D♯-E-F-F♯ . . . and it goes on forever.

There are sharps between everything except B–C and E–F. I can't stress this enough. Memorize it.

Notes and chords move around the fingerboard the same way. If you move a C note 1 fret sharp (up) to C♯, then a C chord would move up the same way. To play a song in C position in the key of C♯, you would move the C chord up 1 fret and therefore move the capo the same number of frets. In this case the capo would be on the 1st fret.

Let's say you know a song in the key of C, and the person with whom you are playing knows the same song in the key of D. To find where you put the capo, you must walk through the following process: Hold a C chord. Move the chord to the right (right-handed players only), or sharp, 1 fret at a time, counting the frets that it takes to move the chord to a D.

It would take 2 frets to do this: C to C♯, C♯ to D. This would mean that you would put the capo on the 2nd fret in order to play in the key of D using a C position. Count the frets needed to move from the key of C to the key of E: C to C♯, C♯ to D, D to D♯, D♯ to E. It took 4 fret places, so the capo would be placed on the 4th fret in order to play in C position in the key of E.

All chords move the same way in order to calculate where the capo should be. Hold the chord of the key that you are presently playing. Think of the key that you want to move to. Count the frets it takes to get there, and move the capo to the fret of the same number. You can make a chart if you need to, but if you practice this process a few times you will not be tied to a piece of paper.

The Microphone

This section was not written to guide you toward purchasing any particular microphone. There are many brands and types of mics available on the market and lots of technical personnel at your local music store to guide you. This section was written to guide you through some of the different types of microphones and how to use them on stage and in the studio. This is something that most of you will probably do at some point, whether it is professionally or just for fun at a jam session. The different means of sound reproduction are the standard microphone, saddle pick-ups, stick-on pick-ups, and condenser microphones.

You will get the warmest, most natural sound from conventional microphones, but they are prone to feedback or boom in the bass if they are not equalized properly. The frequency that will give you the most trouble is the range between the 250 band and the 400 band. This means you should pull down these frequencies on the equalizer or mixing board if a booming, roaring bass is a problem. Moving these frequencies a little can do a lot. Don't pull them down too much, or the bass zone will become too thin or empty-sounding.

You have probably heard people talking about working the mics. It is very important to learn how to control mics for your dynamics and volume. If you don't do it, then the sound person will raise and lower your volume for you. The problem with this is that the sound person doesn't know your show and won't know when to move your channel up or down. Learn to do it yourself.

Test the mic for lead playing. Position the guitar about 3 inches from the mic and point the mic upward, aimed at the treble strings. Make sure there are enough volume and clarity. The sound person will tell you if you are breaking up or distorting the signal by being too close to the mic. Try to stay in this range for your lead playing and fill-ins. Stay about 12 inches away from the mic for playing rhythm. The tone will sound full, and the volume will be about equal to that of the lead. This way, the sound person can leave your volume level alone.

Saddle pick-ups (thin-line type) come in several forms from different companies. This type of pick-up sits under the saddle and uses the downward pressure of the strings on the saddle to press it to the bridge. It has an electric/acoustic sound that is distinctly all its own. The original tone that comes from a saddle pick-up is similar to the tone of the guitar if it were played about a half an inch from the bridge.

Saddle pick-ups have a very sharp tone that needs to be equalized to suit your personal taste. They are very good for raw volume and rarely cause feedback problems.

Stick-on pick-ups can be very good and are usually not too expensive. They can be stuck on the top or permanently mounted inside. Be sure to take your time finding just the right spot for this type of pick-up.

Place the pick-up behind the bridge, about an inch off center toward the treble side. This is a good starting place to test the tone. Plug your cord into an amp. Be sure that the tone settings on the amp are neutral. Play the guitar with the amp volume turned off for a minute or so, then turn the amp up. They should sound very close in tone. If they do not, move the pick-up a little. If the tone has too much bass, move the pick-up a little toward the treble side, and vice versa. If the tone is hollow-sounding, then move the pick-up closer to the bridge.

I have this type of pick-up mounted on my Gallagher "Doc Watson" model. It lies inside the guitar, mounted between the third and fourth strings, sitting on the back-up plate under the bridge. This is where I was able to get a reasonable balance of tone. It still sounds plugged in, but it won't feed back.

The last type of sound reproduction to be discussed is the condenser microphone. It ranges in price from $90 to $400 and is usually mounted inside the guitar in a piece of Styrofoam or with a goose neck. A good condenser microphone is the Shure SM98. Its main purpose is that of a snare-drum mic. Since it was designed to reproduce the attack of a drum, it can take even the strongest guitar player's strum. I point this out because not all condenser mics can handle this strong a strike. Like stick-on pick-ups, condenser mics should be tested in different positions inside the guitar.

I presently use the Mini-Flex stage-model condenser microphone in my Taylor Custom 810. The Mini-Flex is available in three models—club, stage, or studio. Its tone is equivalent to the Shure SM98, it is mounted on a goose neck for optimal positioning, and it is medium priced.

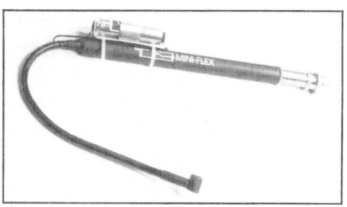

Microphones
Left to right, top to bottom:
Shadow Contact Pick-Ups
Fishman Saddle Pick-Up — Thinline 332
"The Guitar Mic"
"Mini-Flex" #134 — the author's choice
Beyer Dynamic Soundstar MK11

Photo by Tim Everett
Equipment supplied by Murlin's Music World

Bluegrass Back-Up

This section deals with bluegrass rhythm in depth—walking bass lines, the hammer-on and pull-off, and transposing. There are two basic types of time signatures for most bluegrass songs—3/4 time (or waltz time) and 4/4 time.

Let's look at 3/4 time first. This simply means that there are three beats in each measure. This translates into rhythm terms as one bass note and two strums (//), or three strums (///), or a bass walk-in that has three beats to it, or it could mean a bass note–strum–bass note. The choices are almost endless as long as each measure consists of only three beats. Examples of songs in 3/4 time are "Amazing Grace," "The Tennessee Waltz," "Kentucky Waltz," and the list goes on. Keep in mind that "waltz" doesn't necessarily refer to a slow song. Some waltzes move pretty quickly.

It is very difficult in the beginning to keep a steady beat. You can play only as fast as you can change chords. This means that, if it takes two seconds to change from a G chord to a C chord, then there should be the same two-second gap between everything in the song. Count "1, 2, 3" for each beat, and be sure to hit the note or strum on its correlating number.

The following chord chart shows how to hold most, if not all, of the basic chords necessary to play standard bluegrass vocals and instrumentals. My charts are laid out as if you were holding the guitar straight out in front of you, looking at the strings. The peg head is at the top; the end pin at the bottom. The lines going up and down on the chart represent the strings, and the lines going across represent the frets. The dots represent your fingertips on frets that are to be held. The first black line represents the nut, and the numbers above the nut indicate which fingers to use on the strings.

Familiarize yourself with the chords and refer back to this chart throughout this series.

Basic Chord Chart

A
2 1 3
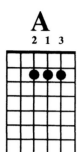

Am
2 3 1
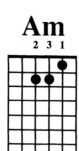

A⁷
2   3

B
X X 2 3 4 1
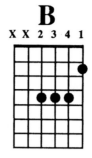

Bm
X X 3 4 2 1
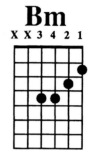

B⁷
X 2 1 3   4
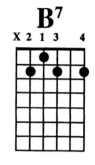

C
X 3 2   1
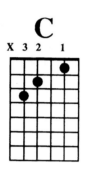

Cm
X X 3 4 2 1
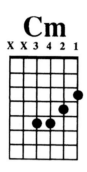

C⁷
X 3 2 4 1
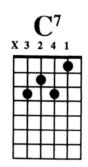

D
X   1 3 2
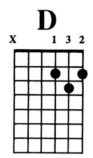

Dm
X   2 3 1
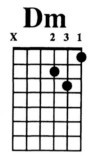

D⁷
X   2 1 3
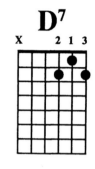

E
2 3 1
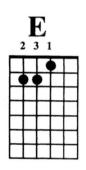

Em
2 3
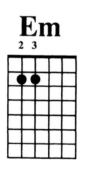

E⁷
2   1
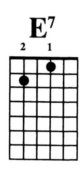

F
X X 3 2 1 1
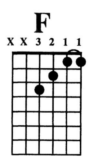

Fm
X 3 4 1 1 1
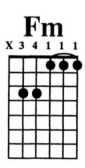

F⁷
X X 3 2 1 1
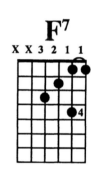

G
2 1   4
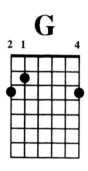

Gm
X 3 4 1 1 1
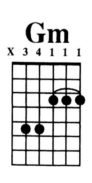

G⁷
3 2   1
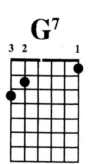

We will use **"Amazing Grace"** as our example of 3/4 time. All of the notes and strums in this example are quarter notes and are to be hit with a down swing. Notice the use of D^7 before all the G chords. The use of 7th chords is a signal telling you that there is going to be a chord change soon. As you go through the series, notice the 7th chords and which chords they go to next.

Amazing Grace #1  Track #4

Now let's take the same song and work in some walking bass lines. Try this example only after you can consistently and smoothly change chords. Notice that all we did to change the rhythm was replace a strum with a bass note that leads us in the general direction of the first note which needs to be hit for the next given chord.

Be sure to count "1, 2, 3" while hitting the notes and strums. Try to tap your foot while you play. If you can tap your foot while counting and playing, you will almost be able to guarantee yourself perfect timing.

Looking at the Am measure (measure 7), you will notice that it has "1 & 2 & 3 &" written over it along with the next few measures. This is to prepare you for a different kind of bass walk. Until this point, every note or strum has been hit with a down swing, directly on the beat. Now we have some eighth notes, or down-ups, on some of the measures. Eighth notes are two notes tied or beamed together, and they are played in the same amount of time that it takes to hit one quarter note. Later on, the eighth notes will also come in groups of four.

Remember this: Two eighth notes are hit down, then up in the same and equal amount of time it takes to hit one regular quarter note or down-swing note. If you are tapping your foot, you can see that your foot is going down then up with the beat. This is the same speed at which the eighth notes are to be played, and also the same direction.

Amazing Grace #2 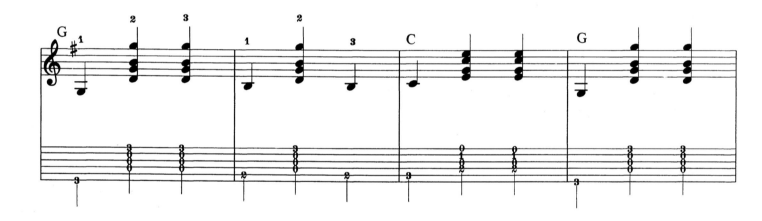 Track #5

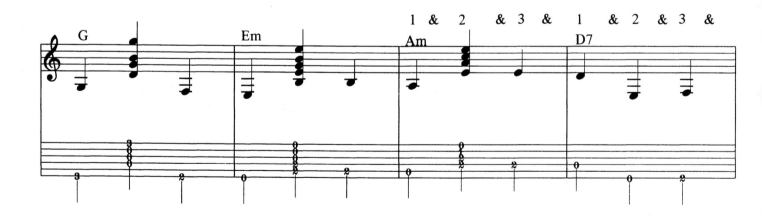

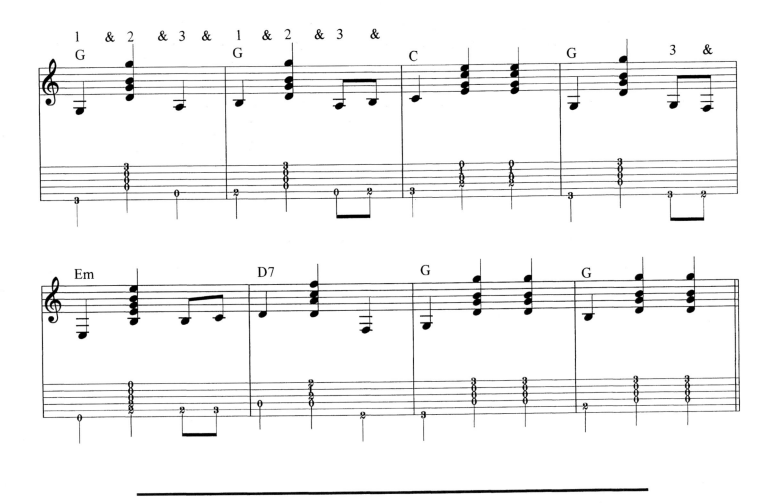

Now we will deal with rhythm in 4/4 time. As we discussed earlier, 3/4 time means there are three beats in every measure—played as a bass note and two strums. In 4/4 time there are four beats in every measure, and that translates into bass–strum–bass–strum.

Let's look at the following chart. It explains how to play the rhythm for the standard bluegrass chords. They are written in order from A to G, and work for all forms of each chord—major, minor, and 7th. The first thing to do is hold an A chord, or any form of A, Am, A⁷. The number "5" means to hit the fifth string. The diagonal line represents one strum. Then hit the sixth string, and follow that with another strum. The four beats necessary to complete one measure are 5 / 6 / .

Look at the B⁷ measure. Now hold a B⁷ chord. You will see that the "6" has a circle around it. As you play through the measure, you should hit the fifth string, then strum. Now move your finger from the fifth string, 2nd fret, to the sixth string, 2nd fret. The sixth string, 2nd fret, is your next bass note to hit, then strum.

C chords and F chords work the same way. With the C chord, you would hit the fifth string, the move your fifth-string finger to the sixth string, same fret. The F-chord movement would be from the fourth string to the fifth string.

Basic Rhythm Patterns for 1st-Position Chords

Now we will put the previous lesson to work. The following song has only the chords written above each measure. It is written in 4/4 time, so there has to be a bass–strum–bass–strum in every measure.

Use the chart to find which bass notes to hit with each chord. Take your time and play it only as fast as the slowest chord change.

The Worried Man Blues

```
G  6  /  4  /  G 6 /4 /  G 6  /  4  /  G 6 /4 /
It |: takes a worried | man    to | sing a worried | song. It |
```

(continue rhythm pattern)

```
C  5  / ⑥ /  C            C              G
| takes a worried | man    to | sing a worried | song. It |
```

```
G            G            G              G
| takes a worried | man    to | sing a worried | song. I'm worried |
```

```
D⁷ 4  / 5  /  D⁷                 G      G
| now — but I | won't be worried | long | ——— :‖
```

Now we will work on 4/4-time bass walks that will lead you from one chord to another. The following bass walks take one measure to complete. They are to be inserted into **"Worried Man Blues"** and also into the following song, **"Lonesome Road Blues."**

Let me explain how they work. The G walk to C takes one measure, or four beats. It replaces the measure directly before the C chord. Instead of playing four measures of G, you must play three measures of G and then the G walk to C. You will find that the walk will shoot you right into the C measure.

You must play the C measure as you normally would— 5 / (6) /.

Next are the three measures of C. Replace the last or third C measure with a C-to-G walk-in. There are five G measures. The last G measure before D⁷ is where you use the G-to-D walk-in. Play one D⁷ measure, and replace the last D⁷ measure with the D-to-G walk-in. Notice the stars above the measures that need the bass-walk substitution measure.

Remember—the bass-walk measure replaces the whole measure before the chord change.

Beginning Bass Walks

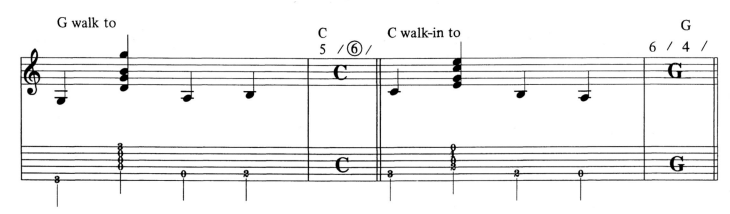

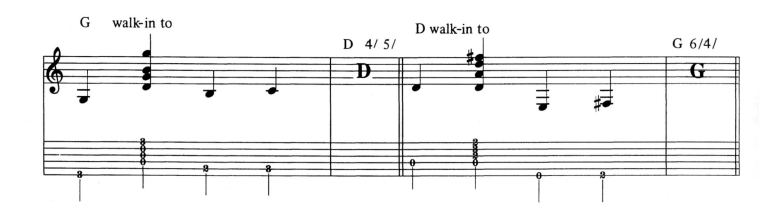

Use the new bass walks in **"Worried Man Blues"** and **"Lonesome Road Blues."** The stars tell you the measures in which to insert the new bass walk.

Lonesome Road Blues

G	G	G	*G⁷	
I'm ‖: goin' down this | road feelin' | bad —— | —— | |

| C | *C | G | *G⁷ | |
| Bad   luck is | all I ever | had —— | —— I'm |

| C | *C | G | *G | |
| goin' down this | road feelin' | bad, lord | lord and I |

| D⁷ | *D⁷ | G | G | |
| ain't gonna be | treated this a- | way —— | —— | |

Here is a more complete listing of walking bass patterns for most of the major chord changes. These bass walks can lead into major, minor, or 7th chords.

Complete Bass Walks for Most Bluegrass Situations

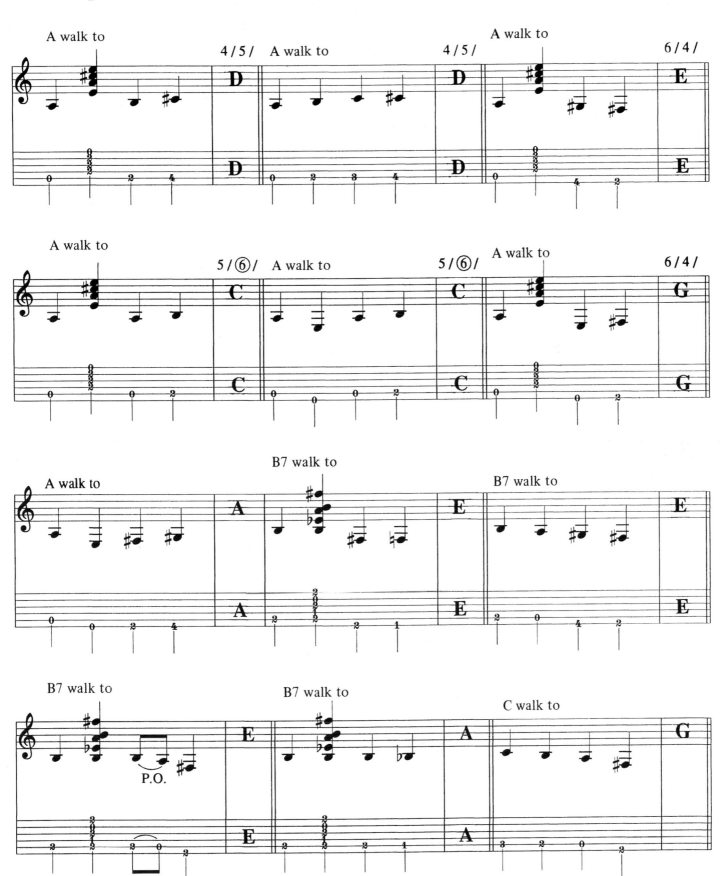

26

There are a couple of bass-walk measures that have hammer-ons and one measure that has a pull-off. The D walk to D and the G walk to G both have the hammer-ons. The way to play a hammer-on is to hit the first note (in both of these cases, the first notes are open strings) and thrust your left-hand finger onto the next note. You will play two notes with one right-hand strike. Your left-hand finger should resemble the hammer of a pistol.

It's not how hard you hammer, it's how you attack the string. The hammer-on will sound mushy if you don't attack the string. You don't have to play the hammer-on fast. If you play it too fast, it will sound out of time. Have your finger cocked and loaded, ready for the strike.

You will find the measure will the pull-off in the B⁷-to-E walk. A pull-off is just the opposite of a hammer-on. When you pull off a note, you strike the fretted string and ease your left-hand finger under the string. Then, with a downward, circular motion, pull your finger off the string. This will cause the second note to sound.

Now it is time to try some of your new-found walk-ins. **"Don't Let Your Deal Go Down"** is a great tune in which to play bass runs. There can be lots of movement because of all the chord changes. Play the walks in this tune and the previous two tunes.

Don't Let Your Deal Go Down

F	*F	D⁷	*D⁷	G	*G	
		‖: Don't let your	deal go	down		

		C	*C	F	*F	
		Never let your	deal go	down		

		D⁷	*D⁷	G	*G	
		Don't let your	deal go	down, sweet	Mamma, 'til your	

		C	*C	F	F	
		last gold	dollar is	gone.		:‖

The patterns for many walk-ins are the same. You hit a bass note, then strum, then hit two more bass notes. These measures can be easily altered to the other type of four-note runs. Hit the first bass note twice to eliminate the strum, and then finish out the run with the remaining two bass notes. This will give you the four beats needed to complete the measure.

You can also change most of the bass runs from 4/4 to 3/4 time very easily. The key to 3/4 time is to have only three beats. Look at one of the 4/4 runs that has a bass–strum–bass–bass pattern. One of two ways to convert the run is to hit only the bass notes. The second way is to hit the first bass note, then strum, then hit the last bass note. Both of these methods will produce the same effect—a 3/4-time bass run.

Play around with these runs until you understand exactly how they are put together and used. Use these runs in all the songs that you know. They may not fit everything tastefully, but you will know how to use them. The hardest part about slipping bass runs into songs is hearing where the run should be placed before you get there. It takes practice.

The following songs, **"Tom Dooley"** and **"Freight Train,"** include all of the techniques that we have discussed so far. These are only the back-up parts, but they show that just playing rhythm can be a good work-out.

Watch for the hammer-ons and pull-offs. You need to hit only the first note of the hammer-on (H.O.) and the pull-off (P.O.). Most people try to hit both of the notes. Just hit one note with your right hand and let your left hand do the rest of the work.

Tom Dooley Track #6

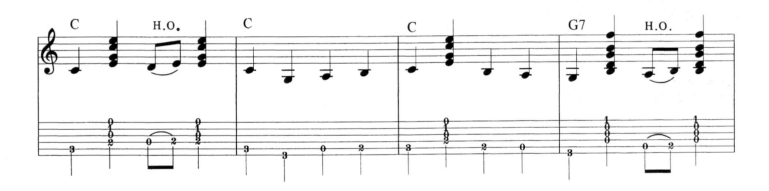

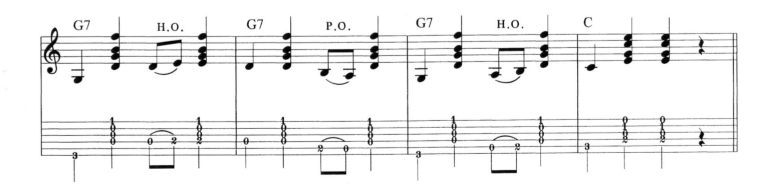

Freight Train

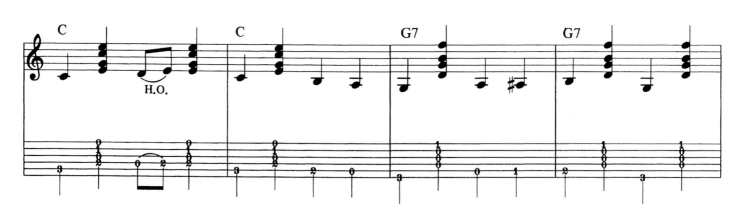

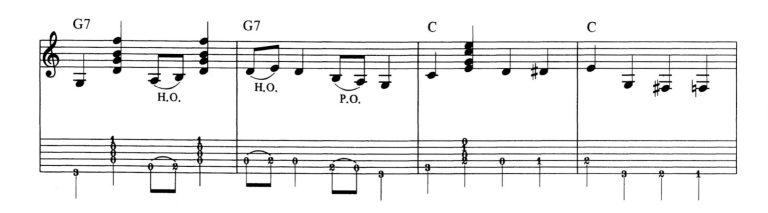

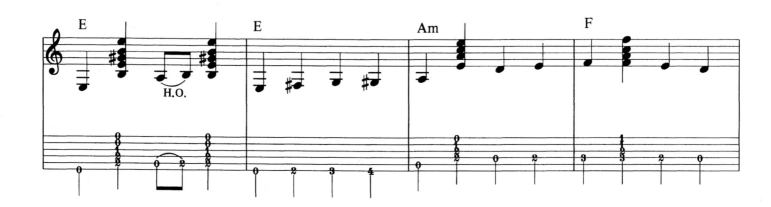

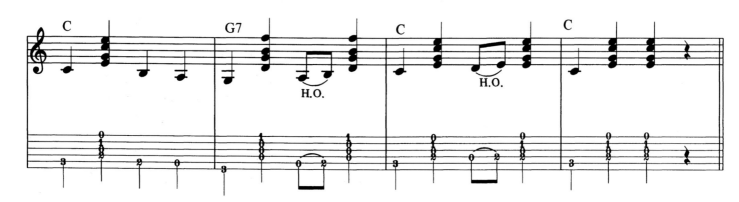

Transposing: Unlocking the Mystery

A B C D E F G, A B C D E F G, A B C...
→ forever.

This little section of the alphabet was discussed earlier. We talked about the ♯s and ♭s. Now we will be working just with the letters. If you were playing a song in the key of G and the person playing with you played the same song in the key of A, what would you do? Stop here and figure it out.

There are two answers. The first is to put your capo on the 2nd fret and play the song in G position. The second is to transpose the song from G to A. Why would you want to know how to transpose songs? Let me throw a snag into our up-to-this-point simplified scenario. Let's say you both start playing in the key of G, but half way through the song it changes to the key of A. Now what do you do? You won't have time to slip on your trusty capo. There is only one answer to this question: transpose. If you have been playing guitar and shying away from this subject—don't, because it is about to open up very clearly.

1–4–5⁷

Memorize these numbers. They represent the chord structure of 85% of the bluegrass and country songs that we play. If you have been playing guitar for a while, you may have noticed that C, F, and G or G⁷ are the three main chords used in the key of C. The key of G has three regularly used chords, also. All of the keys have three main chords.

1–4–5⁷

Let me explain these numbers to you. We have already discussed the three chords in the key of C. Let's work out mathematically how to find them. Start with C and count up four steps alphabetically from and including C:

1 2 3 4
C, D, E, F

C is No. 1, and F is No. 4. Two chords down—one more to go. Now count up five steps starting with C as No. 1.

1 2 3 4 5
C, D, E, F, G

Now we have the 1 (C), 4 (F), and 5 (G) chords. Now make the 5 (G) chord a 7th chord or a 5⁷–G⁷. C, F, and G⁷ are your three main chords to use in the key of C.

A B C D E F G A B C D E F G A B C D E F G...

Find the 1–4–5⁷'s for the keys of G, D, A, and E. "Worried Man Blues" is in the key of G. The 1–4–5⁷'s for that key will directly transpose into any key. Find the 1–4–5⁷'s for the key of G and write the corresponding numbers over the chords in "Worried Man Blues." Now use the 1–4–5⁷'s for the key of C to transpose from G to C. The 1 chord for G will be interchanged with the 1 chord for C. The 4 for G will now be the 4 for C, and so on. If a song in the key of G starts on G and changes to G⁷, it is a 1 that changes to a 1⁷. So, in the key of C, it would change from C to C⁷.

Minor chords will also transpose directly from one key to another. Let us say you are playing a song in the key of G and a Cm chord comes up. A Cm in the key of G is a 4 minor, written as "4-." So, if you were transposing the song from the key of G to C, you would have to find the 4- chord for the key of C. Stop here and figure out what it would be.

Most bluegrass and country songs have three chords. If you are playing rhythm for a standard song in the key of G, you would probably start on a G chord. You are strumming along, and you hear a chord change coming up. If you are not sure which chord is next, don't panic. The choices are the 4 or the 5⁷. You have a 50/50 chance of hitting the correct chord. If you pick the wrong chord, quickly jump to the other choice and file that choice away because that part of the song will come back around again, and you now will be ready for it.

If you played the 4 and the 5⁷, and neither chord sounded correct, then there is an odd-ball chord. An odd-ball chord is usually a 2 or a 6. The 2 or 6 can also be a minor or 7th. "Salty Dog" is a good example of a different type of standard tune. The chord progression for "Salty Dog" is 1/ 6/ 2/ 2/ 5⁷/ 5⁷/ 1/ 1/. For the key of G, that would translate into

G, E, A, A, D^7, D^7, G, G. Each number or chord is the equivalent to one measure in 4/4 time. Musicians call this pattern "going around the circle." It's a standard progression for a rag.

Look back at "Don't Let Your Deal Go Down." It has the same 1–6–2–5^7 progression. Try playing these two rags in different keys. Then try to put in the appropriate bass walk-ins that you have already learned. The previous arrangement of "Amazing Grace" also has some odd-ball chords—the Em (6-) and the Am (2-). These chord changes were not originally written into the tune but are used, in this case, as passing chords or substitution chords.

Remember these numbers: 1–4–5^7, with a possible 2 and 6.

(The answer to the previous question about the 4- chord is F minor.)

The following chart is designed to help figure out the 1–4–5^7, 2, and 6 in any key. The numbers on top of the chart represent these chord changes and any other possible changes that you come across. The vertical column with the "1" on top indicates the key for the letters in that row. The top row of letters starts with a C♯. That indicates the key of C♯. Using the number on top as a guide, you will see that the 1–4–5^{7}s for the key of C♯ are C♯, F♯, and G♯^{7}. Looking nine rows down, you will find the key of F. The 1–4–5^{7}s for the key of F are F, B♭, and C^7.

Go over the chart until you fully understand it. The first vertical column on the left displays the number of sharps (♯) or flats (♭) in the keys.

Master Numbers Chart

	1	2	3	4	5	6	7	8
7♯	C♯	D♯	E♯	F♯	G♯	A♯	B♯	C♯
6♯	F♯	G♯	A♯	B	C♯	D♯	E♯	F♯
5♯	B	C♯	D♯	E	F♯	G♯	A♯	B
4♯	E	F♯	G♯	A	B	C♯	D♯	E
3♯	A	B	C♯	D	E	F♯	G♯	A
2♯	D	E	F♯	G	A	B	C♯	D
1♯	G	A	B	C	D	E	F♯	G
0	C	D	E	F	G	A	B	C
1♭	F	G	A	B♭	C	D	E	F
2♭	B♭	C	D	E♭	F	G	A	B♭
3♭	E♭	F	G	A♭	B♭	C	D	E♭
4♭	A♭	B♭	C	D♭	E♭	F	G	A♭
5♭	D♭	E♭	F	G♭	A♭	B♭	C	D♭
6♭	G♭	A♭	B♭	C♭	D♭	E♭	F	G♭
7♭	C♭	D♭	E♭	F♭	G♭	A♭	B♭	C♭

"Little Maggie" is a tune with some great chord changes. It's in 4/4 time and starts with a 6- chord. In the key of F, that would be a Dm. Try to run through the following changes using the number system.

Yonder Stands Little Maggie

$$\lVert: \; 6\text{-} \; | \; 6\text{-} \; | \; 5 \; | \; 3\text{-} \; | \; 6\text{-} \; | \; 3^7 \; | \; 6\text{-} \; | \; 6\text{-} \; :\rVert$$

I chose the key of F because it is best suited for my vocal part, but the beauty of the number system is that you can choose the key that you feel most comfortable singing or playing in and transpose the song using the chart and number system.

Experiment with the numbers. Play any song, and then write down the chords on a piece of paper. The chord that the song starts and ends on is 99% sure to be the key. Once you know the key, or the 1 chord, you can figure out the rest of the numbers. Write the corresponding numbers above the chords. Next, transpose the song into several other keys. Then tie all the chord changes together with the bass walks that you now know.

Let's go over some of the finer points of this rhythm section:

- *Get familiar with the chords at the beginning of the section. Strum each chord once, then go to the next one. Then randomly switch between all of the chords.*

- *Count to yourself while you begin to play the rhythm parts. Timing is everything. Try to tap your foot while you play.*

- *All notes that are one beat or longer are hit with a down swing.*

- *All eighth notes that are tied together are hit down then up and are played in the same amount of time that it takes to tap your foot down then up.*

- *Play the bass walks slowly and with correct timing. If you have to stop because you missed a note, then you were playing too fast in the first place.*

- *Play the hammer-ons and pull-offs slowly. If you have trouble with the timing of either one, hit them with down-ups until you get used to hearing how they fit together. It's easy to rush hammer-ons and pull-offs.*

- *Learn to use these numbers: 1–4–5⁷, with a possible 2, 6, and 3.*

- *Work with the transposition chart until it is completely understood.*

Arranging Flatpicking Solos
for Bluegrass Vocals

How do I come up with a good-sounding lead to vocals? How do I start picking out the lead? I am asked these kinds of questions all the time. With an instrumental, the melody is already established the way it should be. A vocal's melody should be a simpler task. In general, there are fewer notes to find in a vocal than in an instrumental. The melody notes are usually closer together. Why are melody solos so hard to find? Let's unlock the door to flatpicking the bluegrass vocal.

We will use **"Bury Me Beneath the Willow"** for our first example. The first step is to know the key in which the vocal is sung. We will use the key of G for this example. Listen to the melody on the tape over and over. Try not to look at the accompanying tablature/notes until you've tried to pick out the melody yourself.

When I started to pick out melodies years ago, I would tape a version of the tune (vocals or instrumentals) 15 times onto a cassette, then listen to all 15 repetitions. That would mean that I listened to the tune 30 times. You can remember almost anything after hearing it 30 times. Then I would start to pick out the melody parts that I remembered, referring back to the tape for the parts that I was getting stuck on. I would also write down the process in notes or tablature or a graph of some kind, just so I wouldn't forget what I had already learned. After a little while, I would have the whole tune.

Once the whole tune was "lifted" off the tape, I would play along with the tape until I could keep up with it. Doing this kind of ear study will develop your sense of timing and ear training. Stop here and try to work the first version of "Bury Me Beneath the Willow."

The first version that has been transcribed is only the melody. This is the part that should be playing in your head no matter how intricate your variations become. Keep the chord structure in mind the whole time. You must know which chord is in the background while you play the notes. We will deal more with that soon.

Bury Me Beneath the Willow #1 Track #8

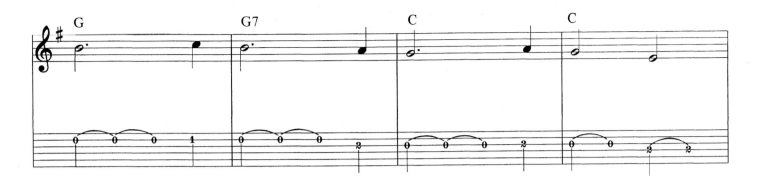

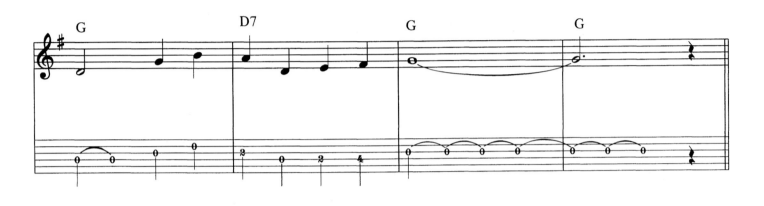

You may find this basic melody a little bland for your taste. Do you remember which chords were the background chords? The next enhancement would be to put some chords into the melody to fill it out. You should notice that the chords are taking the place of only the half notes, dotted half notes, and any other tied notes. Any note longer than one beat can have this type of filler. First find the melody, then fill it up. This is a technique that works with any vocal.

Let's break this theory down. If you have a measure in 4/4 time and in that measure are four quarter notes, then there isn't enough time to enhance the melody with any strums. We will deal with this situation later. If the measure has a three-beat note, it would take one beat to hit it, with two beats left over. Hitting two strums of the back-up chord after hitting the one melody note would take up the slack time of the three-beat note. A four-beat note would have three strums to follow, and a two-beat note would have one strum after hitting the note.

In a situation where there are two whole notes tied together (measures 7 and 8), play the first note, then three strums, and instead of hitting four more strums for the second whole note, hit a standard measure of D, in this case D^7, rhythm—4/5/. The last two measures of G also have been changed so that six strums are not in a row. This would sound too dull and repetitive.

Look at and play through the next version of **"Bury Me Beneath the Willow."**

Bury Me Beneath the Willow #2

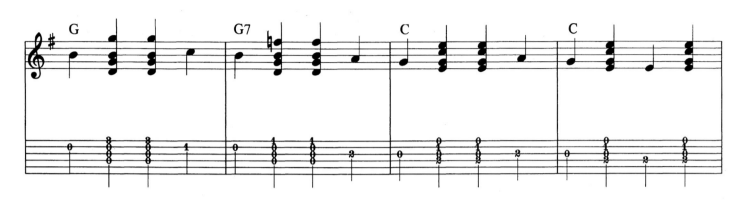

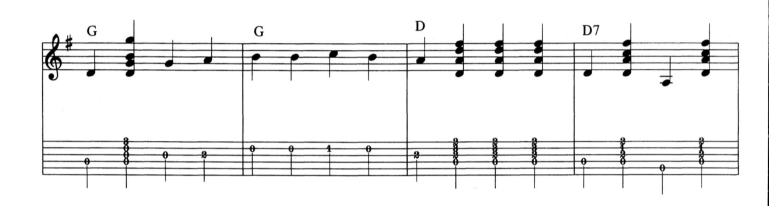

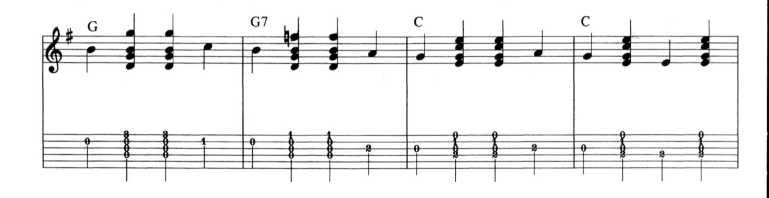

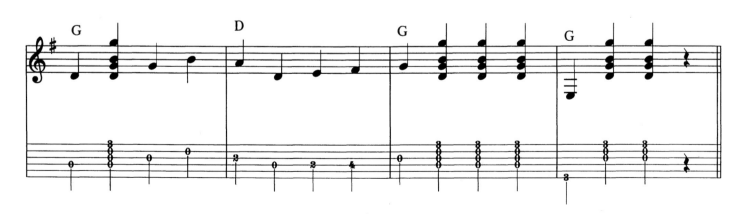

Another form of melodic enhancement is crosspicking. The old style of crosspicking consisted of two down swings and one up swing (1+ 2+ 3+ 4+). This way of picking sounds beautiful when done correctly and in perfect time, but this is hard to do. You can achieve the same effect with more smoothness by using the down-up method (1+ 2+ 3+ 4+) and play faster in less practice time. Either style is correct.

Try the following drill. Play it for the three chords, although any chord will do. Count for each note to ensure proper timing. Watch for the down-ups, and be sure to give the last note a full beat. When you have this exercise smoothed out, you can use it for a warm-up and a right-hand speed drill.

Crosspicking Drill — Track #10

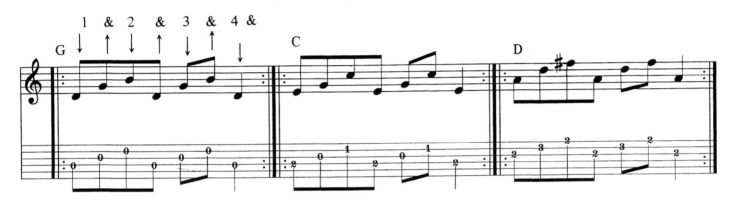

We will now combine the first two versions with the crosspicking patterns to make a third version. The two D-and-G measures discussed earlier will be substituted by the D-to-D and G-to-G bass walk measures that we previously learned.

There are several G measures with stars over them. Look at the first measure of G and hold the chord as shown in the chord chart. It is an F-position chord held on the 3rd fret. If you take an F and move up 1 fret, you have an F#. Moving it up 1 more fret

will give you a G chord held exactly like an F. You will be playing only on the first, second, and third strings, so you don't need to hold the fourth string, 3rd fret, as you normally would for an F chord. Hold this three-string, F-position G chord during every measure that has a star.

Be sure to watch for your down-ups and timing. Go slow and steady at first so that you can go fast later.

Bury Me Beneath the Willow #3

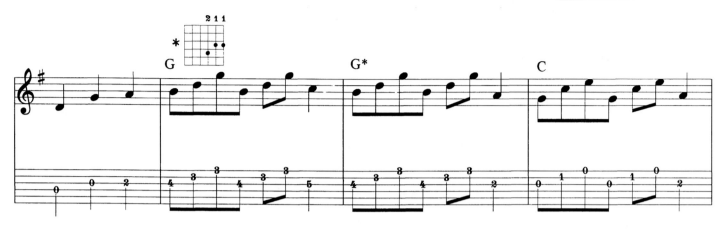

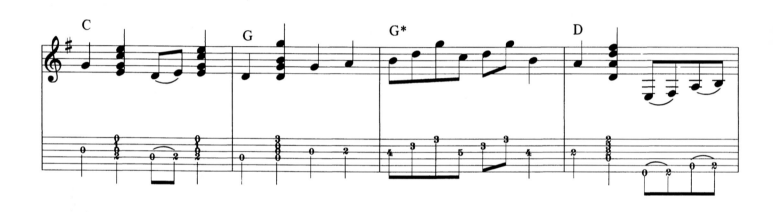

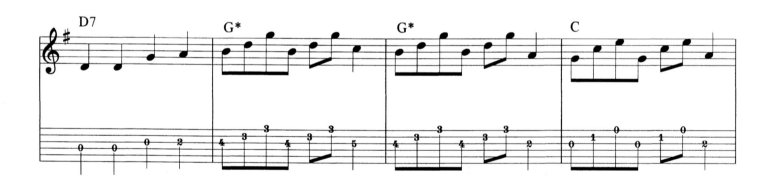

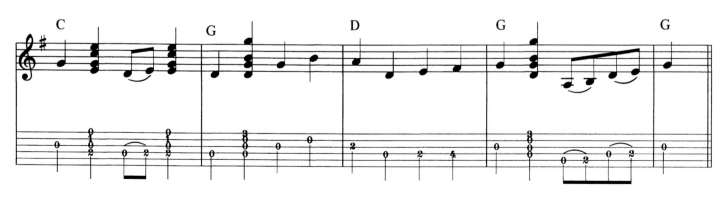

Let's try another tune. We will start with just the melody and build it up into a solid flatpicking solo. Don't forget to practice your rhythm, as well as working out the lead parts. You must always be aware of the back-up chord changes as you play through the lead. Try to use the substitution bass walks in the appropriate measures.

Will the Circle Be Unbroken #1 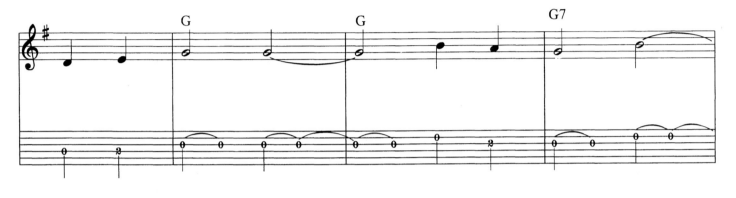 Track #12

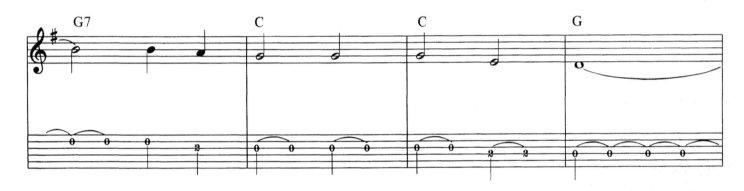

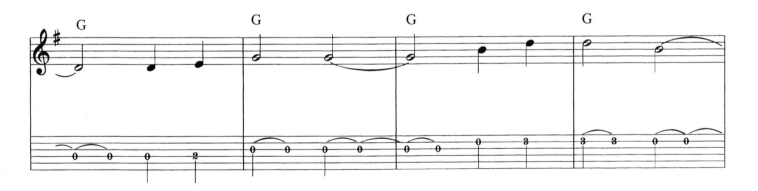

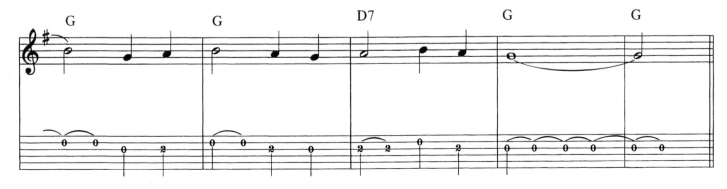

Now we will put the chord structure to use. Keep in mind that all we are doing is filling up the dead space in the half notes by hitting the note and strumming the remaining beat. Notice what has happened to the second, fourth, eighth, and tenth measures. These were all measures that started with a tied note from the previous measure.

Measures 7 to 8 are a substitution run for a G chord to a G chord. Learn to use this run in other similar situations. Notice where it starts and ends. Look for other songs that have the same chord structure, and this run will fit in the same slot.

The last four measures consist of a standard, stock ending run. It is used whenever you have a G to D to G/G situation. You will come across this chord progression many times when playing in the key of G. The last part of this standard run ends with the famous Lester Flatt G run. Be sure to watch for the down-ups.

Try this same principal of finding the bare melody, and then add the strums after any note that is longer than one beat.

Will the Circle Be Unbroken #2 Track #13

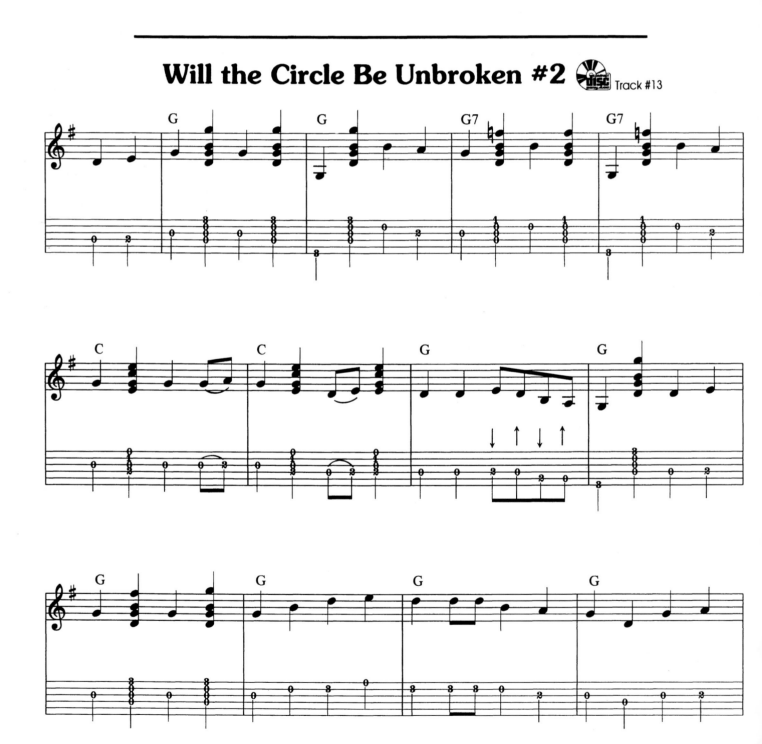

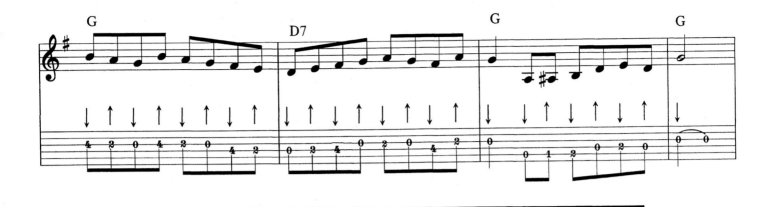

A bluegrass vocal is usually made up of two sections—the verse and the chorus. Most of the time, the solo is adapted to the verse. The process of inventing a solo for the chorus is the same as the verse. It takes time and, like anything else, lots of practice. You must have noticed that the advanced pickers make it look so easy. It's not. They have already gone through what you are trying to do now and have the experience.

The structure of the verse and chorus is usually made up of an even number of measures. Eight, twelve, sixteen, or twenty-four measures are the standard formats. Since it is an even number, either the verse or chorus can also be divided into sections. A good policy of arranging solos is to play the melody for the first half of the tune. This tells the listener that you know how the tune is supposed to go. Then the second section can be left up to artistic interpretation. This means you can jam on the second section as long as it fits the structure.

Most jamming or improvising is made up of stock runs and licks that the player already knows. The only difference in the runs is that the improviser has to arrange the runs so that they tie together neatly. You need to learn as many runs as possible and also understand where they fit, just like you did with the bass walk-ins. The pros call this their "bag of trick licks" or their "vocabulary of stock runs." Learn them from everybody and every instrument.

Let's look at some examples of splitting the solos into two parts—melody, then stock runs that lead from one chord to another.

Wabash Cannonball

Track #14

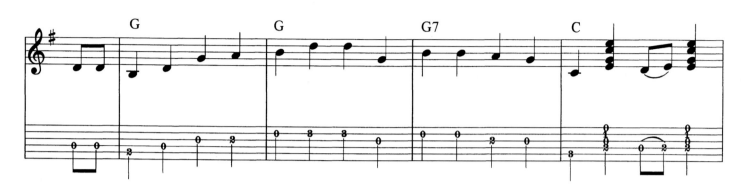

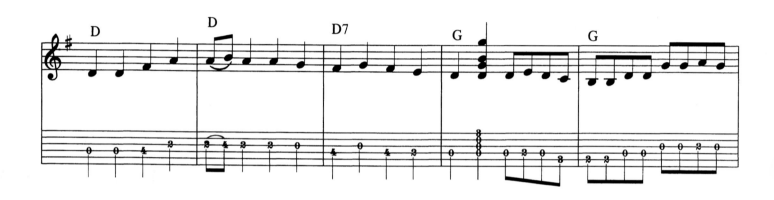

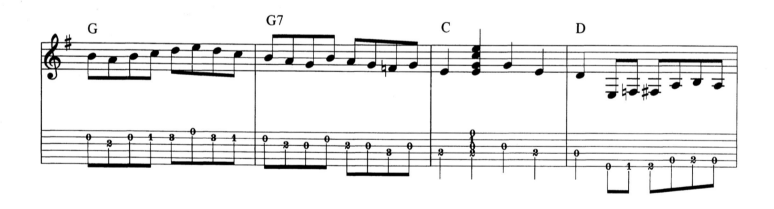

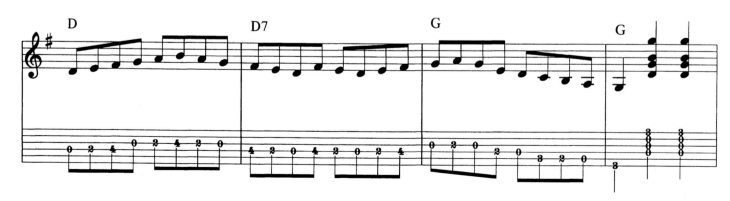

Way Down Town

Track #15

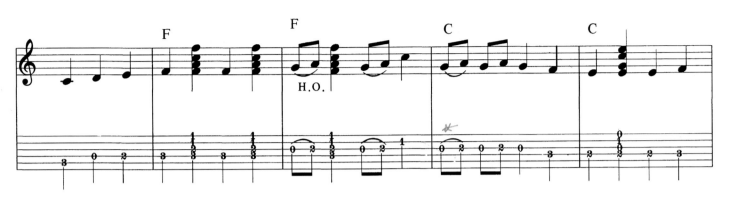

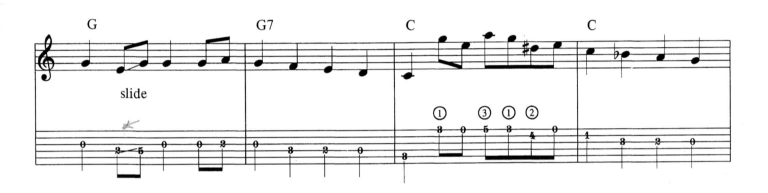

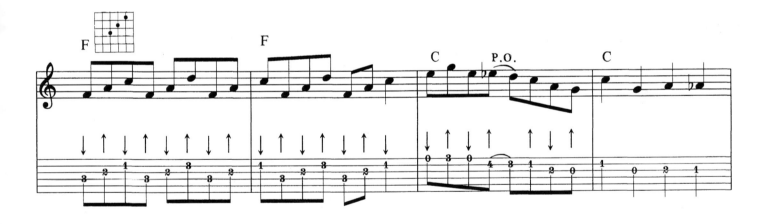

There is some crosspicking in the ninth and tenth measures. Use your first, second, and third fingers to hold this partial F chord, and use your little finger for the D note (second string, 3rd fret). Watch for the down-ups.

Going Down This Road Feelin' Bad

Track #16

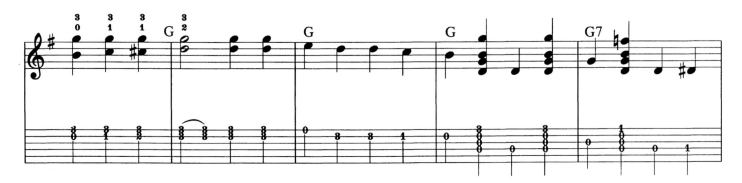

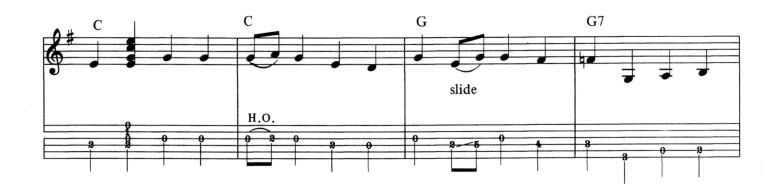

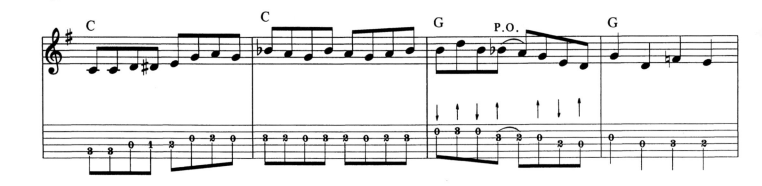

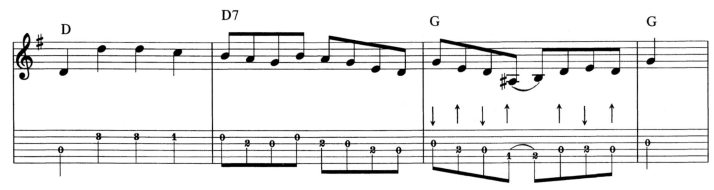

Wreck of the Ol' 97

Track #17

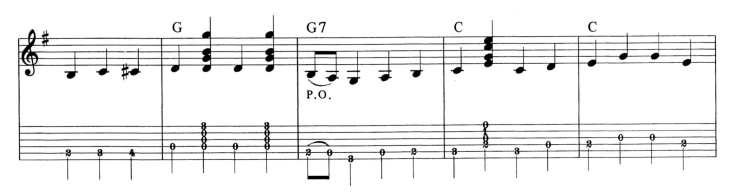

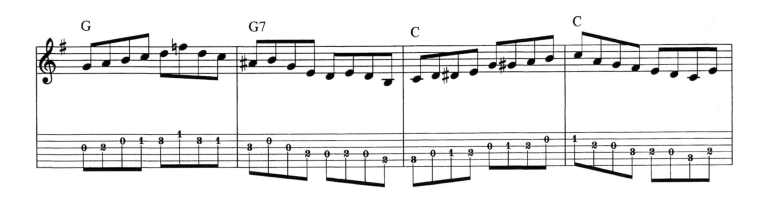

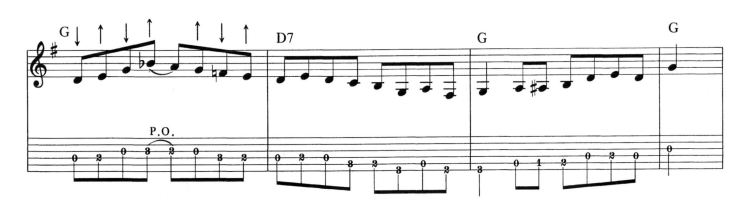

45

Let's go over some of the finer points of this section:

- Listen to the melody over and over until you can sing or hum it.

- Find the key in which it is to be sung.

- Start to pick out the melody notes. They will be in the chord or a fret away from one of the chord notes.

- Keep the chord structure in the back of your mind the whole time you are working on the melody. If you go to the chord, you will find the melody faster.

- After finding the melody, fill up the blank sections with the chords. Any note longer than a quarter note can be followed with the appropriate number of strums.

- Practice the rhythm parts as much as the lead parts. Work in the bass walks.

- Work out the crosspicking patterns. They can be used to incorporate the melody into a filler. Practice crosspicking for all the chords. Use crosspicking for a warm-up exercise.

- When working out an intricate solo, be sure to establish the melody the first time through or at least in the first half of the solo.

- When you are learning these versions or learning from an individual, be aware of the runs that are interchangeable. Learn how they are used, and add these runs to your grab bag of licks and runs.

Arranging Instrumentals from Start to Finish

Flatpicking instruments. This usually paints a picture of a guitarist with a flatpick playing a tune that surpasses the speed of sound. It's not always that way. It can mean playing a waltz, a jig, a hornpipe, and also the hoedowns and breakdowns.

By now you are a smooth crosspicker. You will need the crosspicking to emulate the fiddler's shuffles.

When I arrange an instrumental, I collect all the recorded versions of the tune that I can find that have been recorded by note-worthy pickers, leaning toward the Texas-style fiddlers. You should do the same for the tunes that we will be working through.

There are several different types of instrumental tunes—the fiddle tune, the banjo tune, the guitar tune, the mandolin tune (don't send letters if I've left out any instruments), and the show tune. The show tune is usually a tune that has been adapted to a bluegrass instrument from a source other than bluegrass; i.e., "Sweet Georgia Brown," "Down Yonder," "Lady Be Good," "Temptation Rag," etc. The other types of tunes would mean that the tune was written for a specific instrument but can be arranged so it is playable on a different bluegrass instrument. Fiddle and mandolin tunes work great on the guitar. Most of the banjo tunes are also easily adapted to the guitar.

Arranging the tune is the second most important factor in its playability. You should play at least one straight version of the tune. You must first establish the melody, so this would be your straight version. Play it as close to the melody as you can, putting in runs and hot licks in the center measures and the last measures.

The most important factor in arranging a tune is being able to play the arrangement. Don't make it so hard that you can't get through it.

The center measures are defined as follows. Many standard 16-measure, three-chord tunes in the key of G will probably have two measures of D at measures 7 and 8, and a one-measure D chord at measure 15, ending on G at measure 16. A standard eight-measure tune in the key of G will probably go to D at measure 3 for four beats and at measures 7 or 8 for two beats, then go to G for the remaining beats. These are your center and ending measures that can stray from the melody the first time through. "Old Joe Clark" is a good example of this type of chord structure.

1	2	3	4	5	6	7		8
G	G	G	D	G	G	G	D	G

Measures in 4/4 Time

(This is to be played in the key of A, capo on the 2nd fret.)

Measure 4 is the D chord at the end of the first half of the first part. It is a four-beat D chord. Measure 7 is the split-chord measure. If there is a long D chord in the center of a song in the key of G, then there is a 99% chance of having a short D chord at the end of the section.

We are going to get to some actual flatpicking tunes, but before we do there are some runs that you need to know.

The Lester Flatt G run is probably the most famous run. We will work it out for three different chords—G, C, and D. After you can play the three runs smoothly, move on to the next tune. You should notice that the runs are basically all the same. The tune is a combination of all three runs that make up a bluegrass boogie, reminiscent of "Foggy Mountain Special" by Earl Scruggs. If this tune is played faster, it will turn into a bluegrass breakdown.

Watch for the down-ups.

47

Flatt Runs

Track #18

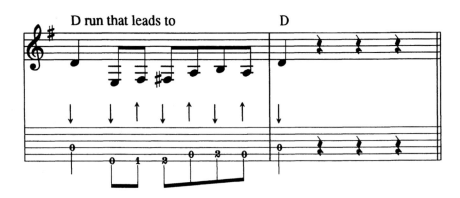

48

Bluegrass Boogie 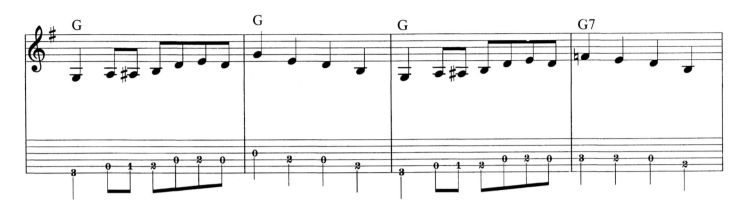 Track #19

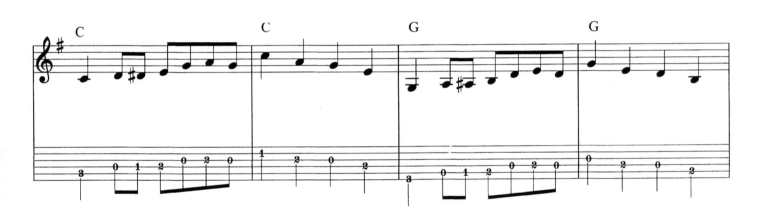

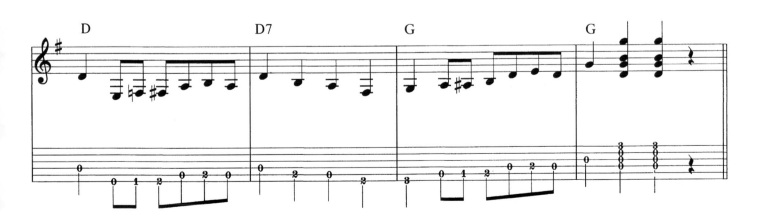

Now we will work on some fiddle tunes, playing the straight melody. The first one is called **"Liberty."** We will play it in the key of C in C position. You must capo on the 2nd fret in order to play this tune with the fiddlers and mandolin players. Practice the rhythm parts as much as the lead parts.

Liberty — A  Track #20

Let's try a little bit of **"Old Joe Clark."** This is a standard fiddle tune played in the key of A. We will work it out in the key of G, so be sure to put your capo on the 2nd fret when you play this tune with a fiddle or mandolin.

Work on the rhythm parts as much as the lead. Use the G-to-D bass walk in the first part and the G-to-F walk in the second part.

"Old Joe Clark" is used by permission from Homespun Tapes Inc.

Old Joe Clark — A  Track #21

Capo on the 2nd Fret
Key of A

51

The next tune we will work on is **"Devil's Dream."** It is made up almost completely of eighth notes. Watch for the down-ups. The main reason we are playing this tune is to get used to playing a whole tune in eighth notes. It is very repetitious, which makes it easier to learn and memorize. Memorizing a tune is very important. If it is only on paper, you will be able to play only as fast as you can read.

The first set of eighth notes repeats three times. Then there is a descending run. You will see a chord chart at the Bm measure. Use your first, second, and third fingers to hold this short Bm chord and crosspick this measure and half of the next measure. Then you

have another short descending run. Next, it's back to the run that was at the beginning. In the | D A | E[7] A | measures is a run that is used to end a song in the key of A that runs through these chords. It is a standard ending (also called a "tag") progression for this key.

The second part (also called the B part) starts with a short A chord (see chord chart). Hold this two-finger A chord and crosspick like you did with the Bm. With the exception of the fifth measure and half of the sixth measure, the B part is exactly like the first part (also called the A part).

Devil's Dream — A Track #22

For lead only

For lead only

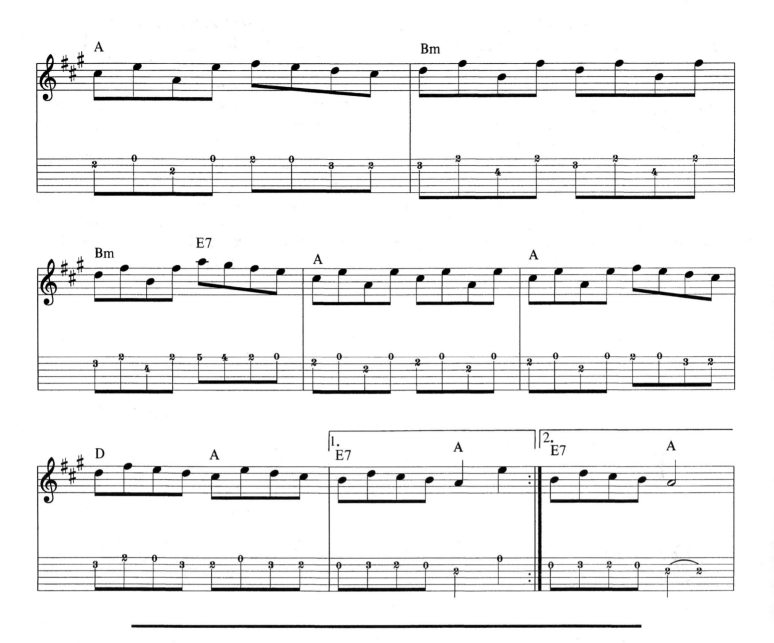

"Sailor's Hornpipe" is a tune I've always had a lot of fun with. It has enough chord changes to make it interesting, which creates a lot of room later for improvising. Measures 4 through 8 in the A part are the same as measures 4 through 8 in the B part. When you get the first part smooth, you will have half of the second part finished.

Look at the first four measures of the B part. There are chord diagrams over each chord change. The G measure tells you to hold an F-position chord on the 3rd fret. You need only the first three strings, so you don't have to hold the fourth string with your ring finger as you normally would with a full F chord. The first finger holds the first and second strings; the second finger holds the third string. You are to crosspick this measure.

The next measure is the C measure. Hold your fingers as illustrated in the diagram—second finger on the third string, third finger on the second string. Moving on to the A and D measures, you will see the same diagrams as the G and C measures. Hold them the same way. This way, your second finger stays on the third string for the whole four measures. There is less to think about when something is organized this way, which means you will go faster. Next is the same run that you learned from the first part. Have fun.

Sailor's Hornpipe — A

Track #23

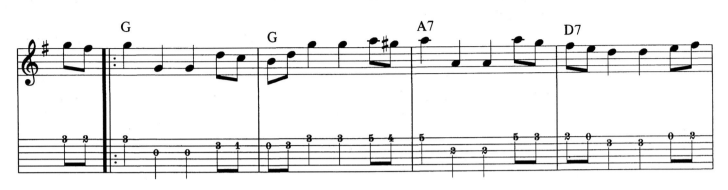

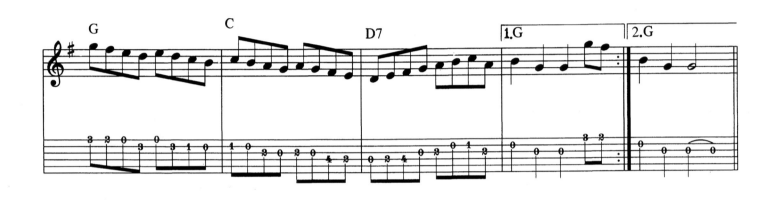

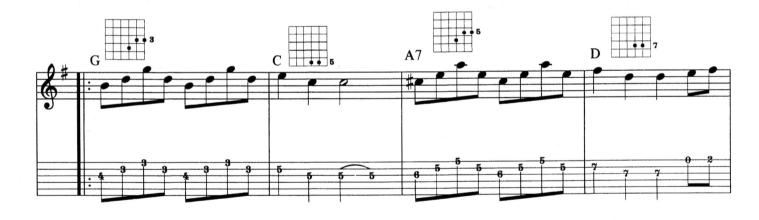

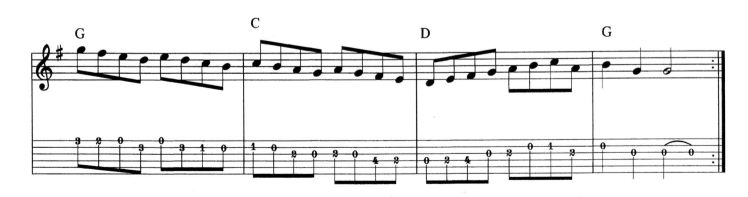

Work through these four tunes until they are smooth before going on to the variations that follow. You need to know and understand the basic versions of any tune before you can understand variations on the same melody. When you can keep up with the tape, it will be time to tackle the variations.

Play through the variation to **"Liberty."** You will notice a few changes—fewer quarter notes and more eighth notes. The first and third measures have been changed to a form of crosspicking. Hold the chord that goes with the measure (see the diagram for the measure). While you play the measure, listen for the melody notes. They are in the same places as the first version.

The second and sixth measures were changed by moving one note sharp and adding two notes to the end of the run. The first and second endings are different. They are runs that are played almost entirely out of the chords. Keep this in mind when working out your own versions. Notice the runs that are now different, and understand what they are doing—the G⁷ run to C, C run to C, C run to G⁷.

Liberty — B Track #24

55

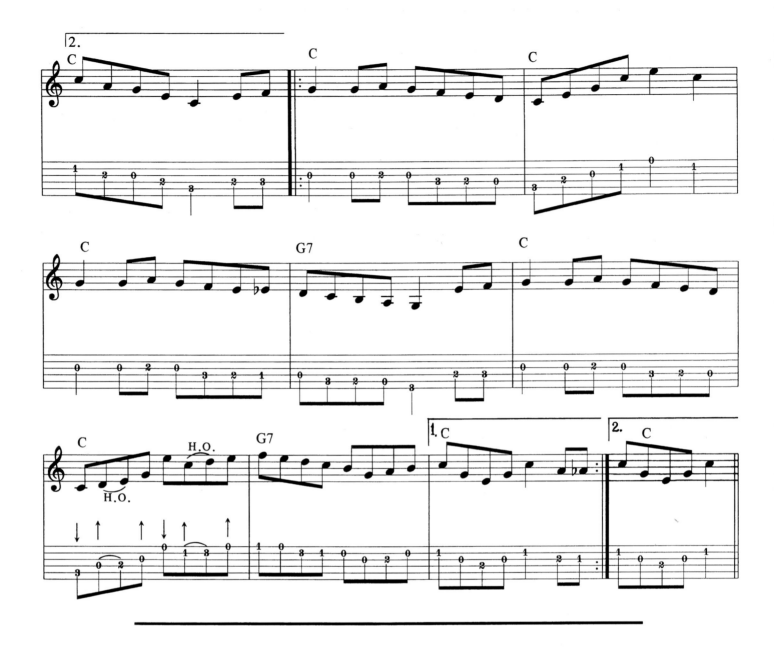

The next variation of **"Old Joe Clark"** was arranged with no open strings in the first part so you can get used to playing in a closed position. You should practice closing off the songs that you already know. If you have known a tune for a long time, then you can hum the melody. This is very important because, as you play any lead, you should be able to hum in your head what you are playing. This will help you keep up your concentration level. If you can hum the tune, then you can find it in a closed position (with no open strings).

Start the tune where you normally would and then exchange the open-string note for the same note closed on another string. Try to work out the second part in a closed position when you fully understand how the first part was closed off. Then, if you play this tune with a fiddle player and can't find your capo, you won't have to say you can't play it or break into a sweat when it comes your turn to play the lead.

Old Joe Clark — B

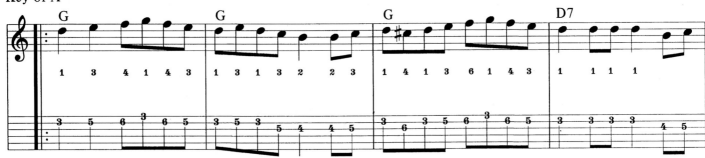
Track #25

Capo 2nd Fret
Key of A

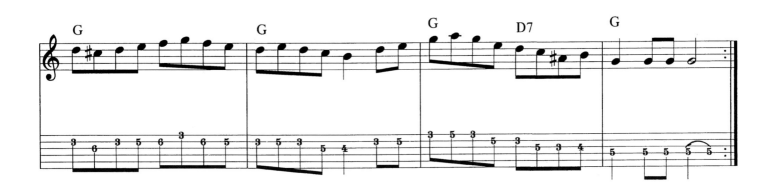

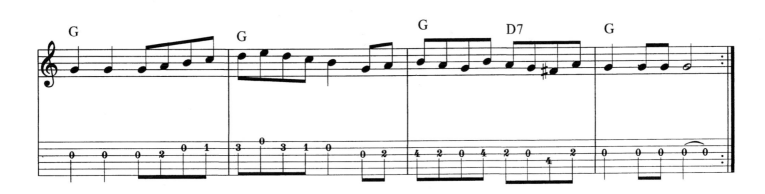

57

"Devil's Dream" is a hard tune to come up with variations for because the melody is so strong, but we found a way. The first Bm run has been almost entirely changed to a closed-position run. This means that it is a run with no open strings. Bm is a substitution chord for D, so this run can be used for either a Bm-to-E or a D-to-E run. Practice this run 1 fret higher and stop at the first note of the second Bm measure. You now have a Cm-to-F run. A Dm-to-G run would be another 2 frets higher, and so on.

All of the first and second endings of this tune are different, and they can all be used in other songs that have the same chord structure. In numbers, it would be a 4/ 1/ 5/ 1 run. This type of run is usually found at the end of a piece. If you were to look at all of the endings as runs and close them all (no open strings), then you would have great ending runs for all of the keys.

Change the first string open to the second string, 5th fret; the second string open to the third string, 4th fret; the third string open to the fourth string, 5th fret; and so on. Now you have a movable run. This is a very important breakdown of how to move runs up and down the neck. If you play the Bm run and don't know how to play the same run for Em, then count through the musical alphabet starting with B and ending with E. Remember that there are no sharps between B and C or between E and F (B → C and E → F). Counting would look like this:

1	2	3	4	5	6	steps from B to E
B	C	C#	D	D#	E	
	1	2	3	4	5	frets from B to E

E is six steps from and including B, so the Em run, like the Bm run that you already know, is six steps from and including Bm. Six musical-alphabet steps are the same as moving 5 frets sharp or up. B to F would be seven musical steps or 6 frets.

Let's stop reading and get on to pickin'! Have fun with "Devil's Dream."

Devil's Dream — B Track #26

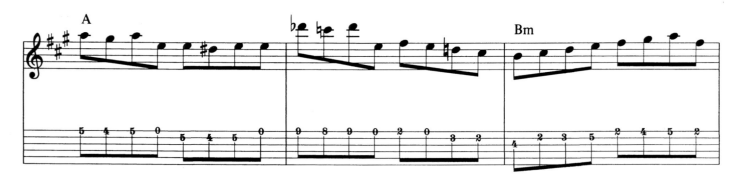

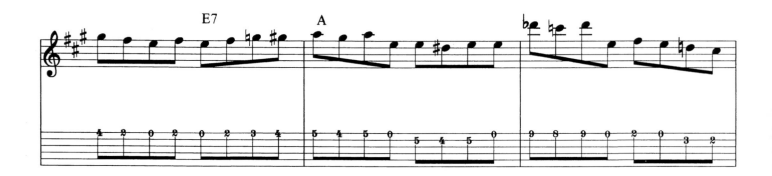

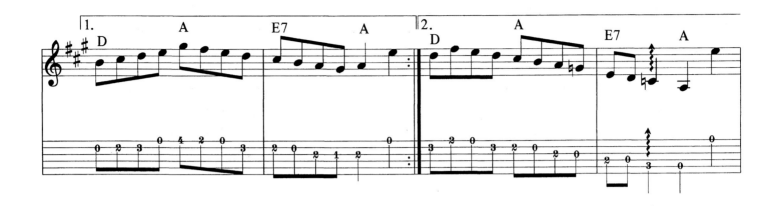

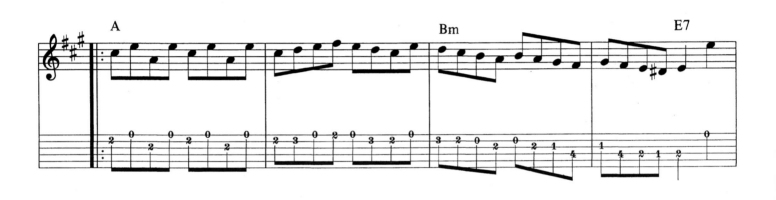

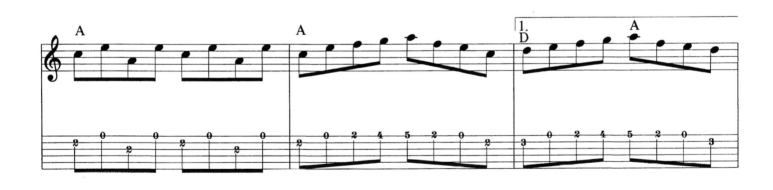

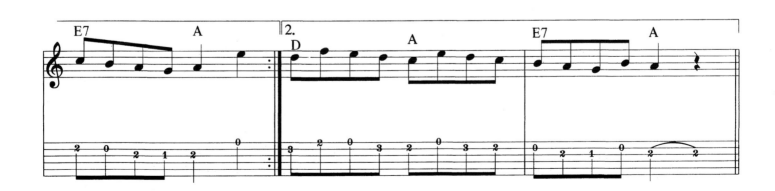

The second version of **"Sailor's Hornpipe"** is an interesting arrangement. I've arranged it with lots of connecting runs. The runs connect from the second G measure through the end of the first D measure. If you were to try this long run in a shorter form, you could start on the G run and break it at the first note of the A measure. You can also start at the A measure and break it at the first note of the D measure or play through the D measure until the first quarter note. The D-to-G runs in the first and second endings are also great interchangeable runs that will fit in many songs, vocal or instrumental.

The A-to-D run in the second part is another great interchangeable run. The last four measures of the second part can be swapped with the last four measures of the first part. They can also be used in many tunes that end with the same chord structure.

Sailor's Hornpipe — B Track #27

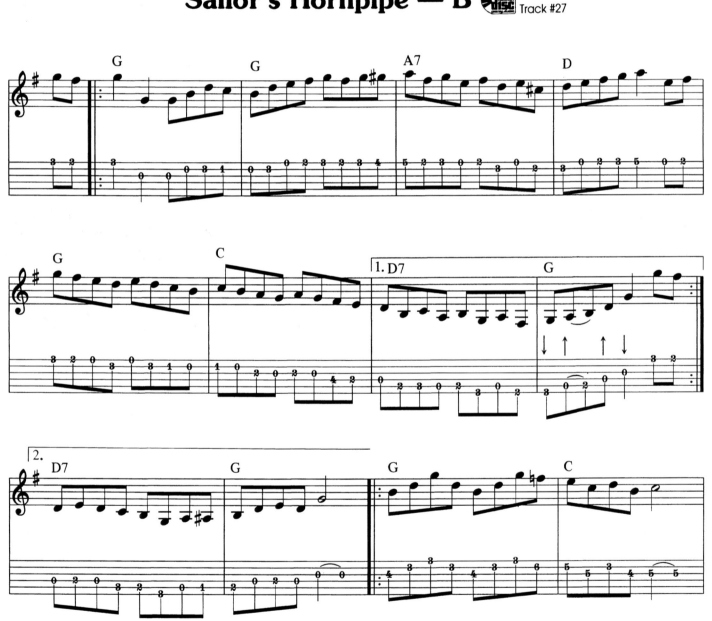

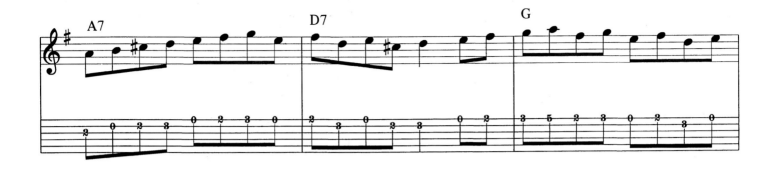

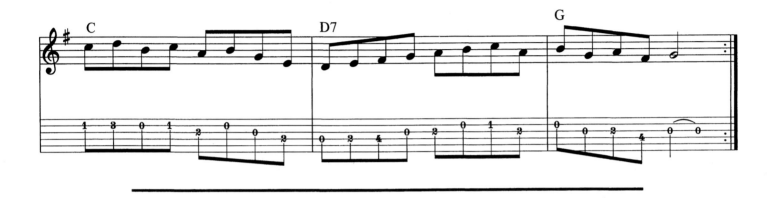

Let's look at some of the finer points of this section:

- Learn the straight melody first and the key in which it is supposed to be played. It is not always necessary to learn it in that key, but be able to move your version into that key either with a capo or by transposing the song.

- When you try to learn a new tune, find all the sources of the tune by various artists that you can. Pick the parts that you like the best from each artist, and merge them into one or two good, solid versions.

- Don't arrange the version so it is too hard to play, given a reasonable amount of practice time.

- Don't rush progress by playing too fast to play cleanly.

- Learn the "Flatt" runs for G, C, and D. You will find a million places in which to slip these runs.

- Watch for the down-ups.

- Learn all the stock runs, turnaround runs, and endings until you can play them in your sleep. You will find yourself using some of these runs in other songs, and you may not even notice that you've done it.

- Learn the stock runs with no open strings. This is the start of playing in any key.

- When you crosspick, be sure to keep the pressure of your finger on the frets as long as possible. Proper crosspicking should sound like all the strings are being hit open, always ringing clear.

- Learn to recognize what is melody and what is an interchangeable run.

- If you hear someone play something that sounds too hard, think this to yourself: "If some person played that—then I can play it also." Maybe not today, but someday soon.

- Try to learn instrumentals right off the records. Tape them over and over until you can hum the melodies, then start to "hunt the notes." I call this "using the Bible method"—seek and ye shall find!

The Flatpickers Who Influence the Flatpickers

We are now going to look at some arrangements of the heavy-weight flatpickers in the music business. As I have told them all, they are my teachers, my heroes, and it is an honor for me to be able to bring part of them to you.

When I was 14 years old, my younger brother Will brought home a Flatt and Scruggs album called *Strictly Instrumental* with guitarist Doc Watson. Will was playing the banjo, and I was playing the rhythm guitar at the time. I had gotten tired of just playing rhythm and didn't know where to go next. When I heard this album, I realized my future direction. I worked out every solo that Doc played on that album and started my Doc Watson record collection. I am still amazed at the control that Doc has. He can play lightning-fast fill-in runs while he is singing. That seems like an impossible separation of the right and left spheres of the brain.

Soon after my introduction to Doc, I began to familiarize myself with the other now-legendary flatpickers—Norman Blake, Dan Crary, and Tony Rice. I found that Dan Crary could play a complete, single-line melody solo while singing. Norman Blake and Tony Rice can play graceful crosspicking backup rolls and interject blinding runs into their vocals with ease. I keep bringing up the ability to play runs and rolls while singing because, as you all know by now, when you first start to flatpick all you can do is grunt occasionally while playing. These flatpickers can play all this, along with tasteful, hot, and powerful instrumentals. We are going to look at these four guitarists in detail.

The versions of the following tunes are similar to the first solos that each has recorded, with the exception of Norman Blake. Norman's first solo for each tune has been transcribed with his permission directly from the recordings mentioned.

Norman Blake

The first picker who we will look at and try to understand is Norman Blake. Norman was born on March 10, 1938, in Chattanooga, Tennessee. He grew up in Sulpher Springs and Rising Fawn, Georgia. His first band, the Dixie Drifters, played the Tennessee Barndance on KNOX Radio in Knoxville. Later, they went to WDOD Radio, and from there to WROM-TV in Rome, Georgia, where they stayed until 1956.

Norman then worked with banjoist Bob Johnson as the Lonesome Travellers. They joined with Walter Forbes in making two records for RCA. In 1959, Norman left these groups to join Hylo Brown and the Timberliners, although he continued as a duet with Bob Johnson in making several guest appearances on WSM's Grand Ole Opry.

At that time, Norman was drafted and stationed in the Panama Canal as a radio operator. There he formed the Fort Kobbe Mountaineers, a bluegrass band in which Norman played fiddle and mandolin. They were voted the Best Instrumental Group, with Norman being voted Best Instrumentalist.

Norman and Nancy Blake

Upon returning to the United States, Norman taught guitar and played the fiddle in a country and Western dance band. He also made frequent trips to Nashville for sessions and to play as a member of June Carter's road group.

In 1969, Norman moved to Nashville to do the Johnny Cash Summer TV show. Around this time, Norman recorded with Bob Dylan on *The Nashville Skyline* album. He was a member of Kris Kristofferson's first road group and did a seasonal tour with Joan Baez. He left Kristofferson to join John Hartford's Aeroplane Band. After that band dissolved, Norman toured with John Hartford for 1½ years. During that time he recorded his first solo album, *Home in Sulpher Springs*. He also received a gold record for his participation in the legendary *Will the Circle Be Unbroken* album. After a nine-month tour with the Red, White and Blue(grass), he left to go back on his own, where he has been ever since.

Norman and his wife Nancy Blake have been touring extensively and have recorded many albums together. In 1989, the Blakes received a Grammy nomination for Best Traditional Folk Recording of the Year for their duet record, *Blind Dog*. One of the tunes we will look at is from this album, along with material from the *Sulpher Springs* recordings.

Norman and Nancy are two of the nicest people you would ever want to meet. If you get a change to get close to either one of them and have a question, be sure to ask because they both will take the time to answer.

We will start this section with a tune from the *Home in Sulpher Springs* album (recorded around 1971). **"Bully of the Town"** is a great example of Norman's ability to play melodically and still deliver a full sound through the back-up rolls and chords. Norman has one of the most fluid right hands in the business. He can fingerpick, play blues, old-time music—you name it, and he can do it.

When you play through a tune like this one that has lots of strums, don't overemphasize the strums by hitting them as loudly or as hard as the melody notes. This will make them sound too deliberate and stiff. Hit the strums lightly, because they are only filler chords and should not overpower the melody. Once you hit a chord and see the same chord coming up again either in the same or the next measure, hold it down to enable the chord to ring throughout the passage.

Play this tune with a loose right hand.

Bully of the Town (Blake) Track #28

Arranged by Norman Blake

The next tune from Norman is **"Done Gone,"** also from the *Home in Sulpher Springs* album. This is more of a straight-line melody arrangement. There are more runs than there are chord fill-ins.

Several measures have high G and D notes that have to be held at the same time. Look at the third measure, which is actually the first measure of the tune. Use your third finger on the first string and your second finger on the second string. Use this same fingering throughout the first part wherever it applies.

Be sure to use the first and second endings in the first part. These are the measures with the bracketed "1" and "2" over them. Start from the beginning and play down to the repeat signs. You will have just played through the first ending. Go back to the repeat sign at the beginning and play through again, skipping over the first ending and playing the second ending.

The last two measures of down-ups in the third part are very tricky. Be careful.

Done Gone (Blake)  Track #29

Capo 3rd Fret
Key of B♭

Arranged by Norman Blake

The next tune we will look at is called **"High Dad in the Morning."** This arrangement came from Norman and Nancy Blake's *Directions* album. It is an old-time tune and is pretty straightforward, but there are still several places to watch for.

In the third Em measure, you will find a dotted quarter note. It should last one and a half beats and is hit with a down swing. The next note is an eighth note which should be hit with an up swing, only after letting the note before ring one and a half beats, then go directly to the next note on a down swing. There are several measures that have this same type of

dotted quarter note/eighth note combination. If the down-ups are not correct, then the tune will be out of time.

The second measure of the third part has a hammer-on in the middle of a nest of eighth notes. It will sound like down-up-rest-up-down. If you have trouble with the timing in this type of situation, then play all the notes as if there were no hammer-on (down-up-down-up) until you get the feel of the eighth notes. Have fun with "High Dad in the Morning."

High Dad in the Morning (Blake) Track #30

Arranged by Norman Blake

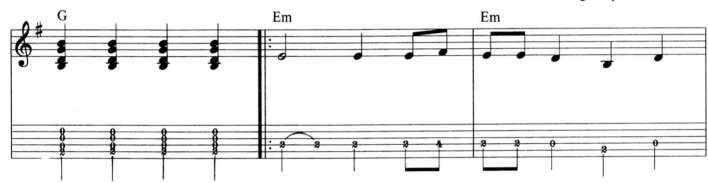

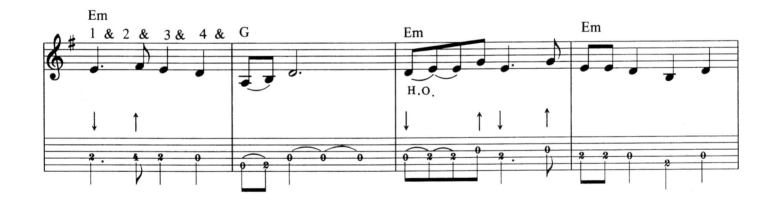

The last tune from Norman is a traditional tune that is played by almost *every* flatpicker—**"Black Mountain Rag."** This arrangement was transcribed from Norman and Nancy's most recent recording, *Blind Dog.*

Norman arranged this tune in G position with the capo on the 2nd fret. Fiddle players play this tune in the key of A, while many guitar players play it in C position with the capo on the 2nd fret. It is a good idea to learn this tune in both G and C positions.

Good luck with this arrangement of "Black Mountain Rag," and be sure to listen to more of Norman and Nancy Blake. See the complete discography for more information.

Black Mountain Rag (Blake) Track #31

Arranged by Norman Blake

Key of A
Capo 2nd Fret

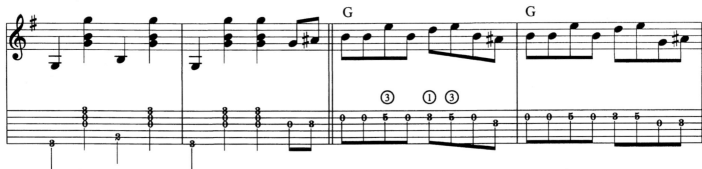

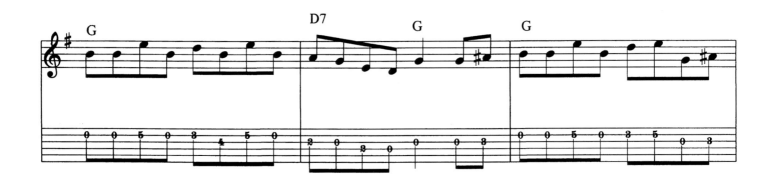

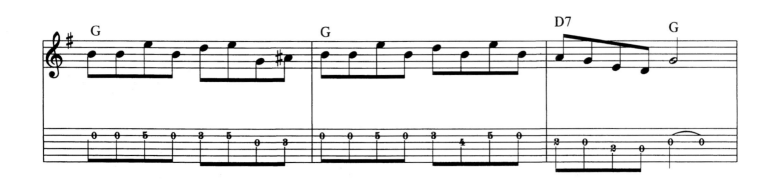

Doc Watson

Doc Watson is the next super picker whom we will look at. Doc is a very versatile musician. He can play old time, bluegrass, blues, jazz, fingerpick, flatpick, and whatever else is needed. As I mentioned before, Doc is the first flatpicker that I listened to and tried to emulate. He will almost always stick to the melody and play only what is necessary. Check out Doc's selected recordings in the discography. If you don't have some of his records, then go to your local store and fill out your collection.

The first tune from Doc is a great example of his style. More notes could have gone into this arrangement, but it could have lost some of the feel. This arrangement is similar to Doc's version on *Doc Watson—Live on Stage*. Doc has a great theory. When he arranges a tune, he will generally stick to the chords, either playing a note then a strum, or playing a melody line that can be found within the chord structure. He also said that, if you get lost while you are soloing, jump to the chord.

We have gone over **"Don't Let Your Deal Go Down"** in the rhythm section—now let's learn how to "pick it." You will notice that almost every measure has some strumming after the melody notes. When you start to arrange your own solos, keep this theory in mind. You don't have to play a thousand notes per song to get a great-sounding solo—you just have to play what is right.

When you play a measure that contains a chord, it is best to hold down the chord at the beginning of the measure and hold it until the next chord change or until you have to release it.

"Browns Ferry Blues" is another Doc Watson classic. There are sixteenth notes, crosspicking sections, "bluegrass blues" runs, and the good old "Lester Flatt" runs.

The first measure starts off with a slide, second finger, on a down swing then up on the second string, 3rd fret, with the first finger. Leave these two fingers down because, in the second measure, you will need a partial G chord using your first, second, and third fingers. Your little finger will hold the E note (5) on the second string.

These little hints will get you started. The fingers are marked and so are the down-ups. Pay close attention to all of the markings. They will help to ensure a smooth ride through this solo.

Don't Let Your Deal Go Down (Doc)  Track #32

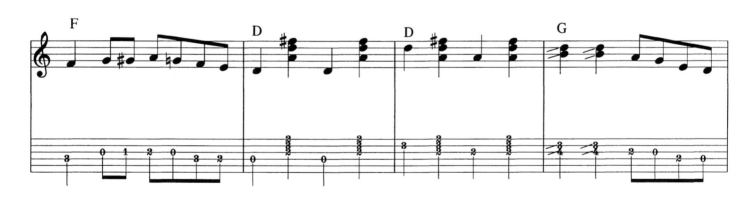

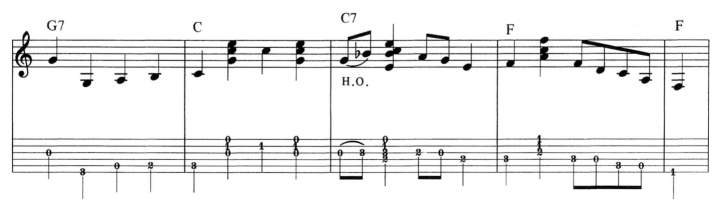

Browns Ferry Blues (Doc)

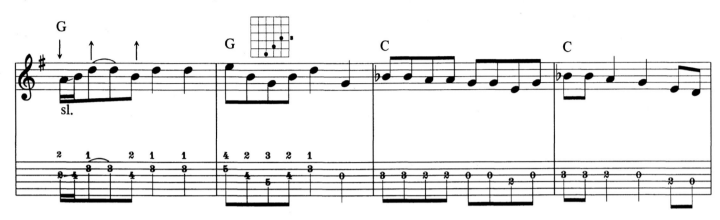

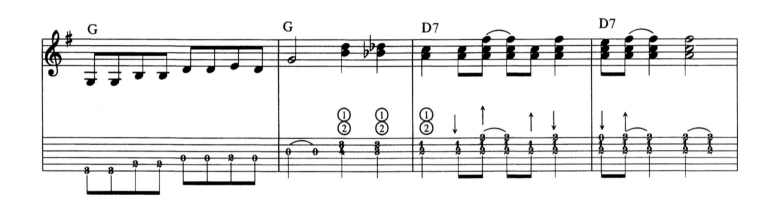

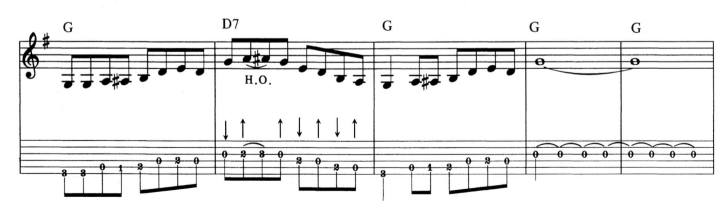

The next two Doc-style tunes are fiddle-tune instrumentals. **"Salt Creek"** has a few tricky spots. It starts with a slide using the second finger. Hold this note down while you hit the open third string. The note from the slide will sustain and overlap onto the open strings, making this type of run sound smoother.

The second part starts with your first finger holding the first string, 3rd fret. The second measure is tricky because of the timing. There is a dotted eighth note, then a single eighth note. To practice this type of syncopated timing, it is best to fake a down swing after the dotted eighth note, then swing up and hit the flagged eighth note. Measure 6 of the second part is the same.

Be sure to use your capo on the 2nd fret when you play this tune with a fiddle or mandolin player.

Salt Creek (Doc) Track #34

The first part of **"Billy in the Low Ground"** is straightforward with the exception of measure 7. Follow the arrows to play this measure correctly. Swing down, fake the next up and down, then hit up, all the time keeping your wrist moving like a pendulum on a clock.

The second part has the same type of tricky timing. Measures 3 and 4 of the B part have to be played by faking certain swings. It is syncopated more than the measure in the first part, so take your time and be sure to get it right.

Billy in the Low Ground (Doc) Track #35

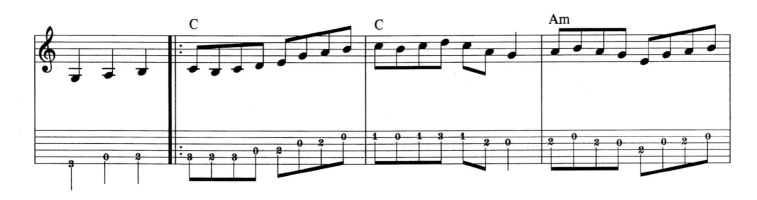

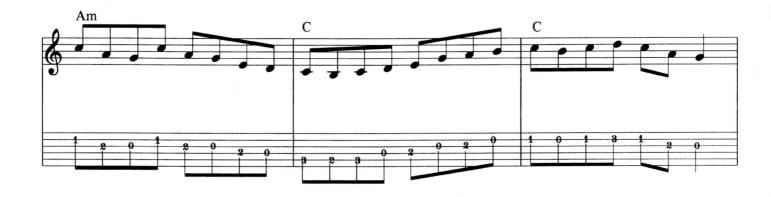

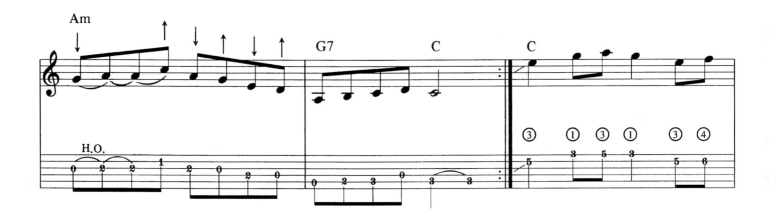

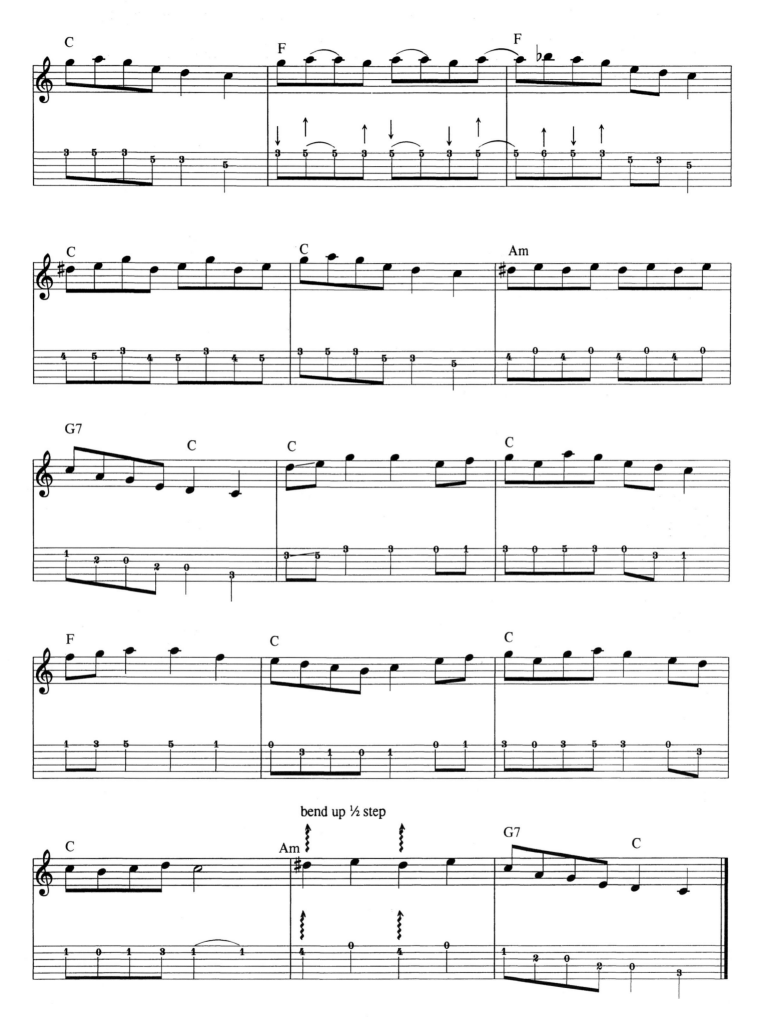

Tony Rice

Tony Rice is a very fluent flatpicker. He plays the ballads to the blues with a modern approach. His left and right hands work together as if they were one. This is evident in any of his blazing solos. The slower ballads that he arranges are full of contemporary chord riffs and changes. The solos are always played with taste and innovative ideas. Look at Tony's discography for some of his recordings.

We will look at the traditional style of Tony Rice. The first tune that has been arranged in his style is **"Temperance Reel,"** also called **"Teetotalers Reel."** The first part has one particularly tricky measure. Measure 7 has a "two-ups-in-a-row" segment.

The second part has an interesting first measure. Hold your fingers like the diagram shows. It looks and is fingered like a D^7 that starts on the second string. This is an alternate fingering for an Em chord. Hold this position for the complete roll.

Measure 3 of the second part has two ups in a row. Watch out for the timing.

Measure 5 has a quick slide from the 4th to the 5th fret on a down swing, then up on the first string open. This should take the same amount of time as a regular down-up. Each part is played twice.

The next tune arranged in the style of Tony Rice is **"The 8th of January."** This is a fast-paced fiddle tune that is played mostly in the key of G but is also played in the key of D. This is the key we will use.

There are many hammer-ons and pull-offs in this arrangement. Here is the general rule for hammers, pull-offs, or slides in groups of eighth notes: Whatever direction you hit the note which starts the hammer-on, pull-off, or slide is the same direction you will hit the next note after the hammer-on, pull-off, or slide. That's why, when looking at the arrows over the eighth notes in some of the measures, you will find two up swings or two down swings in a row. Keep this theory in mind as you play through this version.

Learn the last four measures of the second part as a "stand-alone" four-measure C run that will interchange in other tunes with the same ending chord structure.

Temperance Reel (Rice)

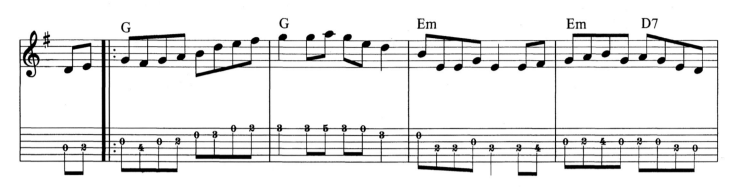

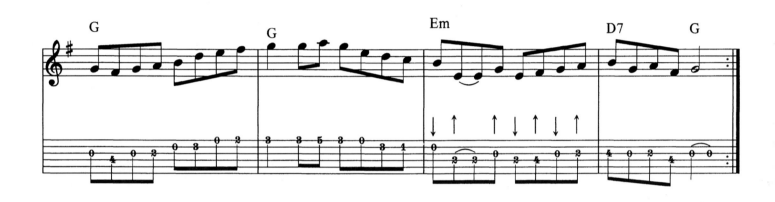

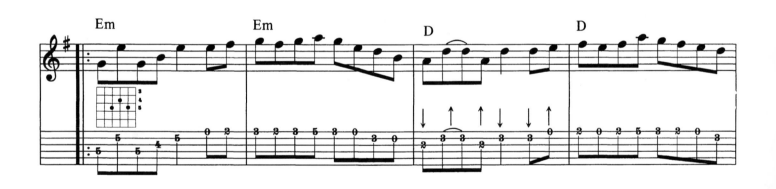

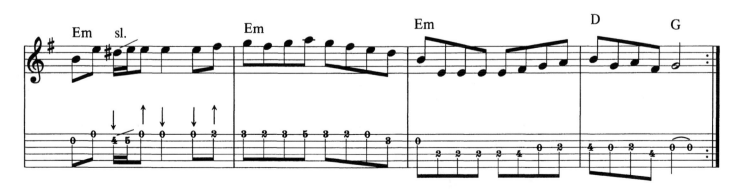

The 8th of January (Rice)

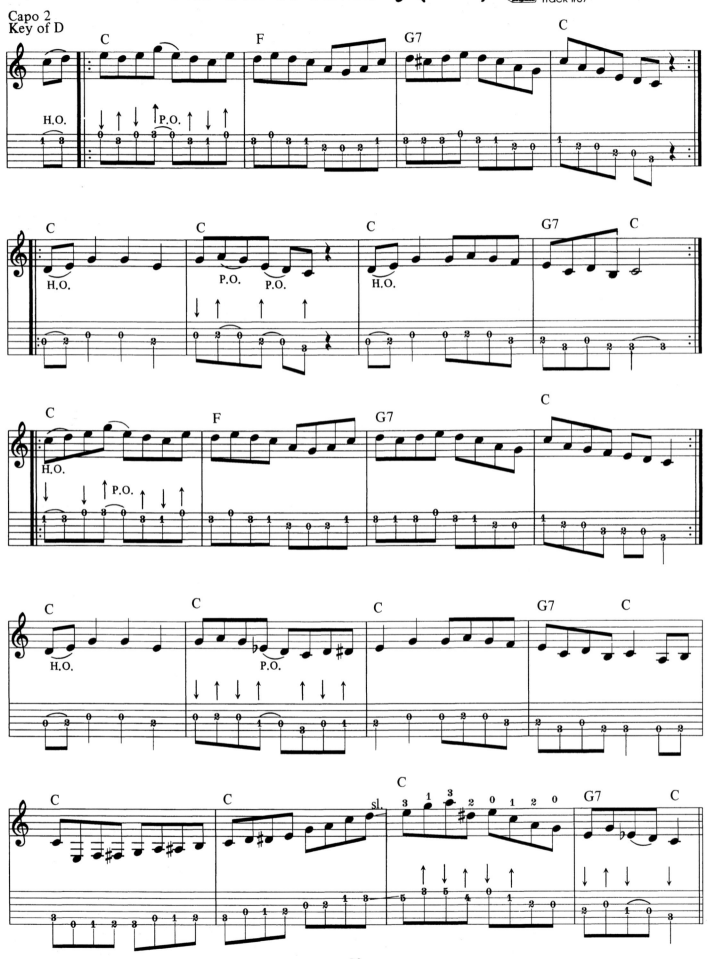

"Cattle in the Cane" is another tune that has tied eighth notes in the first part. The second part starts with your first finger barring across the first, second, and third strings, making a short Am chord. This is a great-sounding, old-timey tune with a hook. The hook, or the difference between this tune and many others, is that the first part is in a major key and the second part is in a minor key. Tunes like these are more interesting to me, and I can play them for hours without getting tired of hearing them. Watch the down-ups.

Cattle in the Cane (Rice) Track #38

The last tune in the style of Tony Rice is **"The Red Haired Boy,"** also called **"Little Beggar Man."** This is a tricky arrangement, and in it are some classic Tony Rice-style runs.

Measures 1, 3, 5, and 9 all have the same "two-ups-in-a-row" situation. Measure 8 has a third-finger slide from the 3rd fret to the 4th fret.

Measure 15 has some tricky fingerings. Use the open strings to give you time to jump between the different positions.

The end of measure 26 is the beginning of a "Floaty" run. Use your first finger to slide from the 1st fret to the 3rd fret, maintaining the pressure while you hit the first string open. Hit the 3rd fret again, maintaining the pressure while you hit the 5th fret, third string. Keep the third string fretted while you hit the second string open. You should have two notes ringing. Your little finger will fret the fourth string, 7th fret, while the 5th fret and the open string are still ringing. It sounds complicated, but in theory you should have at least two notes ringing at all times in a "Floaty"-type run.

The last four measures of this arrangement are an interchangeable G run. See how many songs in which you can make this run work. Be sure to use your capo when you play with the mandolin and fiddle pickers.

Red Haired Boy (Rice) Track #39 Track #40

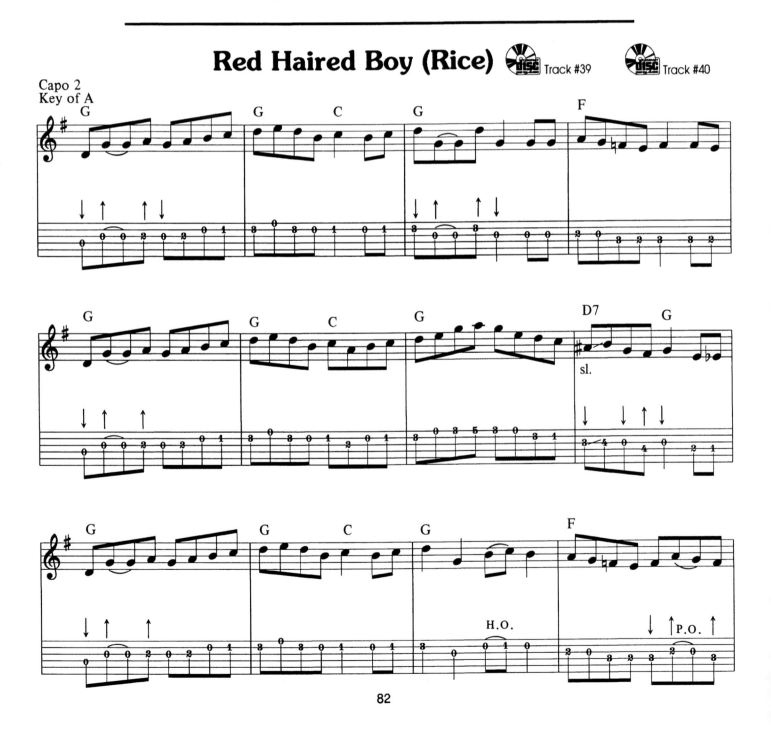

Dan Crary

There have been many articles written about the next flatpicker. He is a very distinguished and articulate person, whether he is playing guitar or teaching a workshop. Dan Crary is a premier guitarist, recognized internationally as one of the founders of the "flatpicking" style. Dan is the first flatpicker I know of to record a completely instrumental flatpicking fiddle-tune type of album, called *Dan Crary—Bluegrass Guitar*. It may still be available and should be in every flatpicker's record collection. I listened to that record until I had all the runs and licks memorized. I wasn't satisfied until I could play everything on it.

Since that time, Dan has recorded many albums, his latest work being *Take a Step Over*. Be sure to check it out. Look in the discography for more of Dan Crary's work.

Dan Crary

The first tune from Mr. Crary is **"Dill Pickle Rag."** It is his first solo of the tune and can be heard on his *Lady's Fancy* album.

There are six pick-up notes that lead into measure 1. Be sure to hold the 3rd fret, first and second strings, with your first finger on both strings.

Watch for the down-ups throughout the first part. Proper right-hand technique is the only way to play the tricky syncopated measures.

The second and third measures of the B part are repeated throughout the section. For measure 2, you must keep the fourth string fretted with your third finger while your little finger and first finger do the work on the second string. Measure 3 is the same, except your second finger frets the note on the fourth string. Be sure to keep the fourth string ringing for the whole measure.

The C part starts with a slide into the 3rd and 5th frets with your first and third fingers. Start the slide from the 2nd and 4th frets. Measure 2 of the C part has some tricky fingerings. Watch out.

Measure 9 of the C part is a great one-measure interchangeable run for a C chord. Measure 10 is an interchangeable C run that leads to F.

The last four measures of the C part are connecting runs that can be taken in their entirety and put into other songs with the same ending progression; i.e., "Beaumont Rag," if played in C position.

Dill Pickle Rag (Crary) Track #41

Arranged by Dan Crary

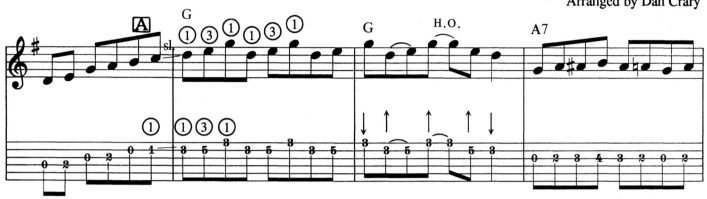

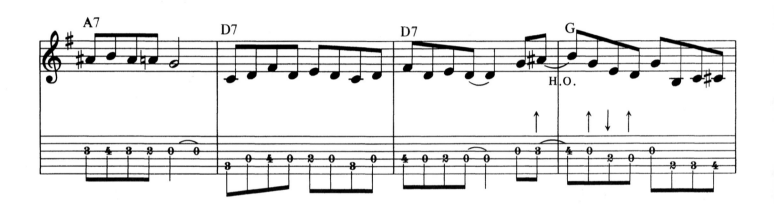

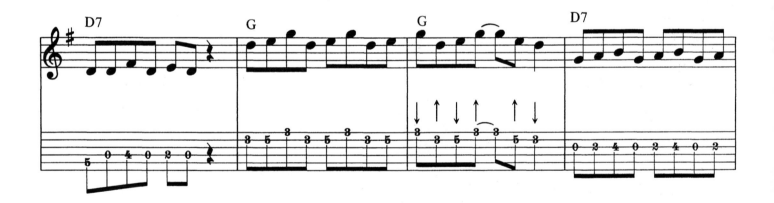

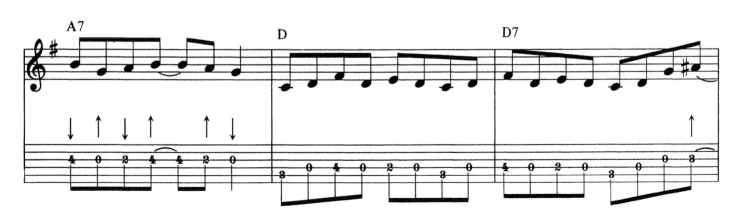

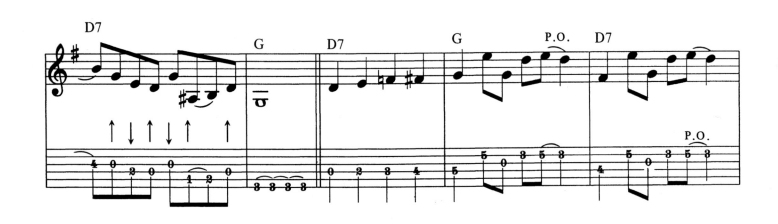

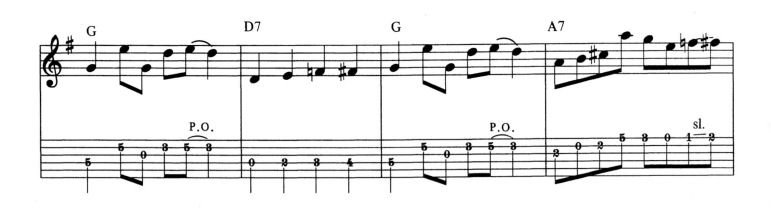

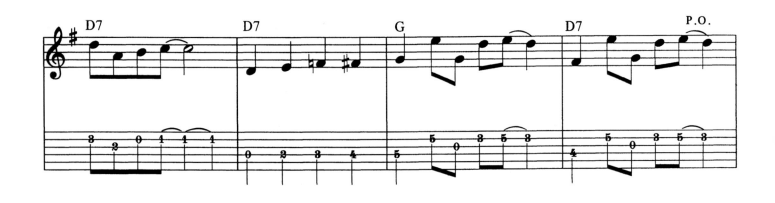

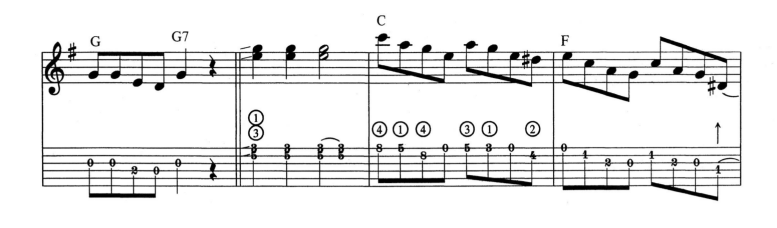

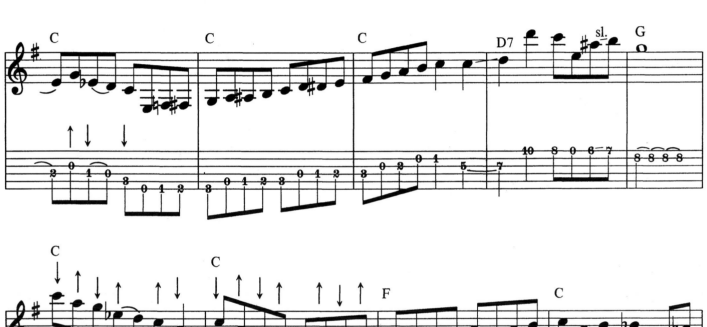

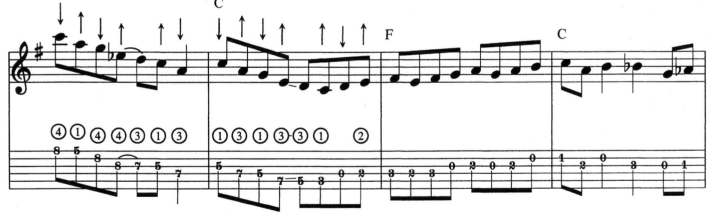

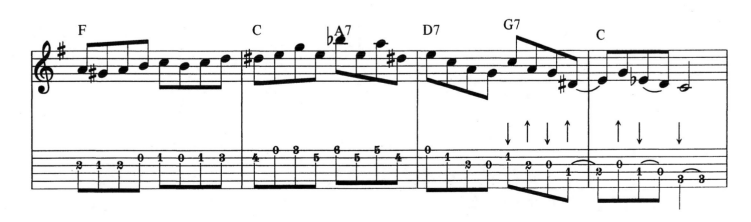

"Flop Eared Mule" is our next tune from Mr. Crary. It is found in a medley with "Done Gone" and "Crazy Creek" on Dan's *Take a Step Over* album. Some of the sections are a bit tricky, but as a whole you should be able to learn this arrangement pretty quickly.

Measure 4 has two sets of hammer-on triplets. Use your first and second fingers for both sets. When practicing this measure, be sure to play seven notes in a row to get the feel of this type of passage. The seven notes include the six notes of triplets and the D note (3rd fret, second string). Follow the arrows in measure 9.

The second part is a fairly straight-ahead section. Have fun with it.

Flop Eared Mule (Crary) Track #42

Arranged by Dan Crary

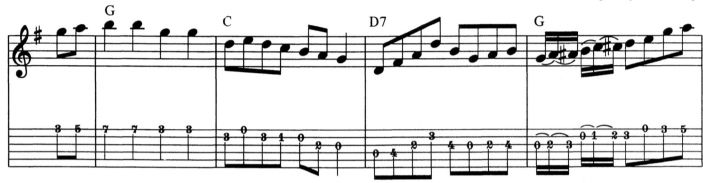

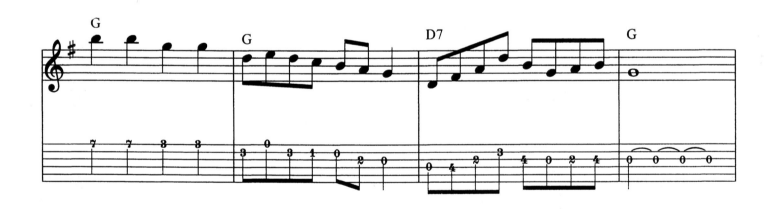

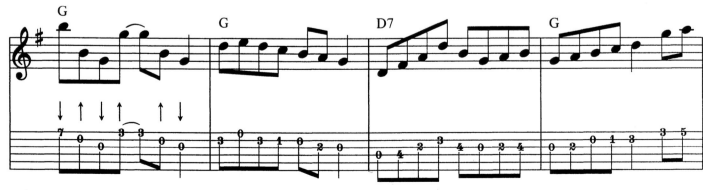

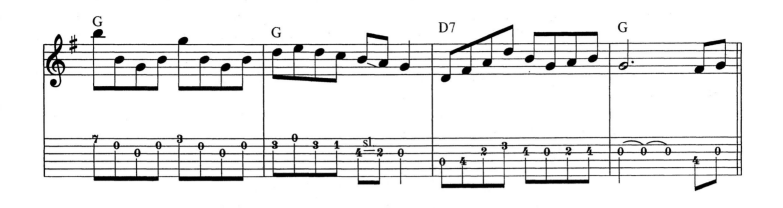

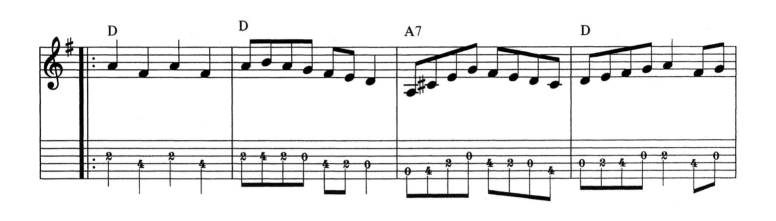

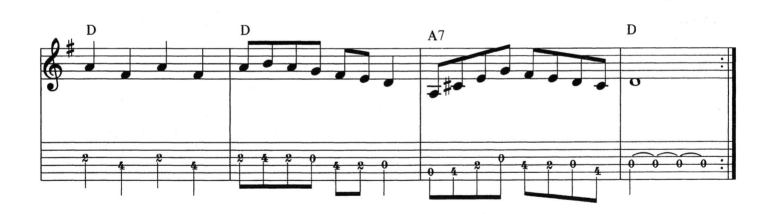

The last tune by Dan is the second tune in the medley described earlier. **"Done Gone"** has always been a fascinating tune for me. Dan played it in the key of G as opposed to Norman's arrangement in the key of B♭. It should prove interesting to see how both of these flatpickers perceive this tune.

There are many hammer-ons, pull-offs, trills, and triplets—a lot of the power, technique, and phrasings for which Dan Crary is most famous. Watch out and have fun.

Done Gone (Crary) Track #43

Arranged by Dan Crary

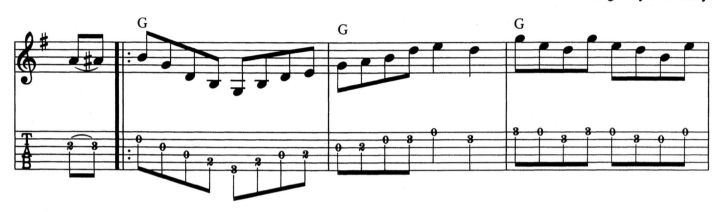

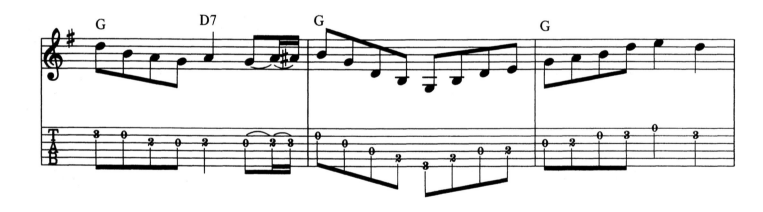

The Steve Kaufman Approach

"Steve Kaufman has long been a formidable name in the world of hot guitar picking. He is the only three-time winner of the National Flatpicking Championships held each year in Winfield, Kansas. Steve is not only a sensational flatpicker but is a dedicated and superb guitar instructor."

Happy Traum
Homespun Tapes

"Steve is one of the best young flatpickers in the country. And along with his flair for the hot and flashy, he has some additional ammunition like power, clarity and musical taste."

Dan Crary

"The tone and phrasing are excellent and most important—the melodic sense is superb. You certainly set some high standards for all of us to aspire to."

John Hartford

"The playing is as always, strong and confident—your style is engaging in a way that draws the listener in and holds their interest—this is a rare feat."

Pat Flynn

"Steve Kaufman can stay firmly within the traditional bounds of guitar picking. His playing, however is anything but predictable; Steve manages to combine the taste of Norman Blake, the strength of Dan Crary and the imagination and verve of Clarence White. The lift in his playing is wonderful, the execution perfect, the ideas attractive and well balanced. In other words, Mr. Kaufman is definitely a man to be reckoned with."

Duck Baker

The kind words that you've just read have been written through the years about my style and about me. They are printed here to help illustrate some of the points and fundamentals that I've strived for while in my learning process, a learning process that never ends. Let me try to explain some of my philosophies and how my style developed.

I started playing guitar (flatpick style) at the age of 14. I would listen to the recordings of Doc, Norman, Dan, and Tony over and over. Eventually I was able to "lift" the tunes by ear from the records. By the time I was 17, I was able to mimic and play along with almost everything that Doc, Norman, and Dan had on record.

I point out playing along with records because this is when I developed my speed and volume. Cleanliness came later. I would turn the volume up very loud so that I would be sure to stay in time with the record. In order to hear myself, I had to hit the notes very hard, which in turn helped develop my volume. Speed and volume usually don't go together. You must practice both speed and volume separately and together. One will be sacrificed for the other if you don't practice correctly, so be sure to work on both.

Doc taught me to play the melody and the "less is more" theory. To quote a fiddle player from whom I've learned many things, "A tune is a tune because of the tune." Play the melody. If you play runs and licks that don't have any significance other than that they are hard to play or that some hot picker played them, then you may destroy the tune/melody for what it really is—an individual tune. Just playing runs and licks will make all the tunes sound the same.

Norman Blake taught me to flow. When you watch Norman you will see that his right hand never stops. He stated in a recent Homespun video that he was taught to make his right hand appear to be shaking off water. Keep your right hand flowing (down-up). This will help you keep your timing steady.

Norman and Doc taught me the use and need for crosspicking. You will find some crosspicking in almost every vocal that they play and in some of the instrumentals. Norman also taught me the use of "double stops"—playing the melody and complementing the melody note with a harmony note.

Dan Crary taught me to hit the notes like you mean it, with confidence and power, combining this strength with the use of dynamics. The only problem I have found with this is that, if you make a mistake, you are going to make a *loud* mistake. This is when you have to just look up and smile. You have to be able to laugh with, not at, yourself. After all, the bottom line is that you are playing guitar for fun.

Tony Rice and Clarence White taught me the use of syncopation. They taught me to experiment with the timing and play around with different phrasings. They showed me how scales and runs, other than the standard bluegrass type, can and will fit into traditional music.

I am proud to say that Norman Blake, Dan Crary, Tony Rice, and Doc Watson are all great people, great performers, great musicians, and, through their recordings, great teachers. Go to their shows and buy their records.

Now we will look at how I would develop a tune, using **"St. Ann's Reel"** as an example. We are going to play it in C position with the capo on the 2nd fret. This will put the song in its correct and standard key. This tune is written in C position because of the interchangeable runs that occur in the second and third versions.

I have written out three versions of this tune; the first version is the straight melody. It is as bare as I could make it and still make it a challenge. It shows how the melody should be played. The first rule in arranging is to establish the melody. I am using the standard chord structure for this tune with no substitutions—yet.

When you work out a new tune, do the following: Work the chord structure out first. Hum the melody while you play the chords. You need to know exactly what the melody is at any given point while you play the chords. Look for ways to have the chord structure help you find the melody. The melody notes are more than likely to be found in the chords themselves.

An example of this is measure 3 of the first part of this tune. Hold a partial F chord as it is charted. You will notice that the melody is right in the chord. Measures 2, 6, and 8 are easily played while holding a C chord. Learn this straight melody version, and practice it until you can hum the melody.

St. Ann's Reel #1

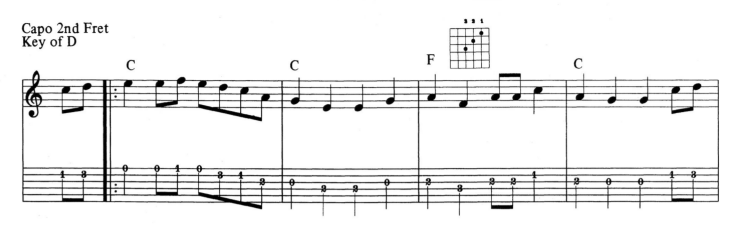

Capo 2nd Fret
Key of D

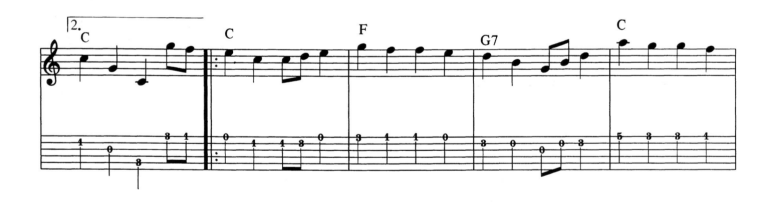

The second version of **"St. Ann's Reel"** demonstrates in greater detail the use of chord positions to help find and vary the melody. Work slowly through the following breakdown of the first and second parts. Try to analyze what I have done in order to merge melody with variance.

The following breakdown of an improvisation is, in my case, done in a split second or, as we say, "on the fly." These next two versions are improvised solos that are written and broken down so that you can see the thought processes involved subconsciously when a picker improvises.

Measure 2 has been changed to a descending run that connects the first measure to the second measure and incorporates the melody in the run.

Measure 3 is now a roll or a form of crosspicking with the F chord. It fills the whole measure and also uses the melody notes.

Measure 4 has a hammer-on to the A note instead of just hitting the A note.

Measure 7 makes full use of the F and G chords by substituting two sets of eighth notes in the form of a roll, instead of just playing four quarter notes. You can still hear and see the melody notes in this measure.

Measures 8 and 9 finish the first part by continuing the roll or the theme established by measure 7.

These last two measures are a great example of playing out of the chords.

The second part has been changed to a series of straight-line melodic runs that interconnect between the chords and the melody. The back-up chords have been altered a little. Two of the F chords have been changed to Dm. Dm and Dm^7 are substitution chords for F, also called "relative minors." Dm is the relative minor of F. If you compare an F chord with a Dm chord, you will see that they have two notes in common. This is what makes them relative. Another useful thing about relating Dm to F is that an F run can substitute for a Dm run and vice versa.

The last measure of the second-part first ending is a run that should be set up out of the C chord. First hit the fifth string, 3rd fret, and keep this note down while you hammer on the fourth string. Hold down these two notes while you hit the third string, and then onto the second string. When you finish this little run, you should be holding a C chord. If you are not, then the tones will not ring or sustain.

Sustain is the key word. Make all your notes ring like open strings—don't settle for dead notes. Do all you can to figure out why some of the notes that you play are not ringing as long as they should. Analyze yourself as often as you can stand it. Tape yourself so you can hear your mistakes and fix them.

St. Ann's Reel #2

Track #45

Capo 2nd Fret
Key of D

96

The third version of **"St. Ann's Reel"** is arranged in the Texas "play-yourself-into-a-corner-and-try-to-play-your-way-out" style. You will find a lot of weaving in and out of the melody, but subliminally it is always present.

Beware of the down-ups in measure 3. Hold the partial F chord as it is charted. The right hand does all the work. The left hand moves only the second finger.

Measure 19 has two sets of hammer-on triplets. One set of triplets is equal to one beat. There is neither a gap in time between the two sets of triplets, nor is there a gap from the last note of the triplets to the first note of the next measure. When you practice this run, be sure to play seven consecutive notes before there is a time gap.

Measure 30 also has two sets of triplets. The difference here is that these triplets are hammer-on/pull-off triplets. These are also called "trills."

Good luck with all three versions of "St. Ann's Reel."

St. Ann's Reel #3 Track #46   Track #47

97

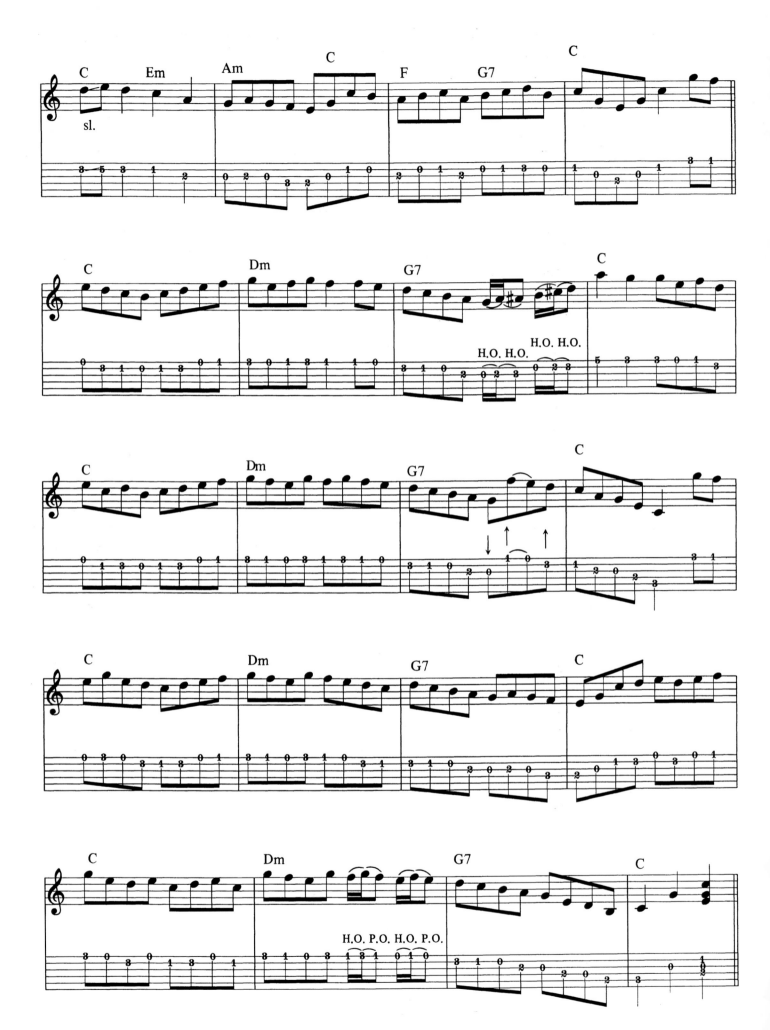

98

We have covered many things in this guide to flatpicking. Some things that we haven't discussed yet are things like jam etiquette, practice habits, and my all-around general thoughts:

- *Set aside a regular time every day for practicing. It must be an everyday, hands-on experience. If time is running short one day, just play some drills or one song ten times.*

- *Many of my beginning students ask me the standard question, "How long will it take to learn to play this guitar?" I don't answer by telling them to practice an hour every day or by saying that after six months they will be good enough to jam with someone. My answer is deeper than that. Everyone is different in ability, but I answer this way:*

  There is a predetermined amount of time that it will take everyone to reach his or her own goal. Let's say it takes 2500 hours total practice time to get from the beginning stage to the advanced/professional level. If you practice a half hour a day, which is 3.5 hours a week, then it would take 5000 days or 13.69863 years to reach your goal. If you practice an average of 2 hours a day, or 14 hours weekly, then it would take 1250 days or 3.42 years. It is not probable that you could average 14 hours every week for over 3 years—you have to be dedicated to a schedule. Your personal practice habits can change these numbers.

- *Don't practice mistakes. You will only dig yourself deep into a hole that is hard to climb out of.*

- *Don't practice if you are tired. Your concentration level won't be what it should be. The best time to practice is in the morning before the worries of the day are on your mind.*

- *When you jam with other people, use your ears. Here is a theory that I wish everyone would consider: If you can't hear the person playing the lead, then **you** are playing rhythm too loudly. If seven guitarists are in a flatpicking jam, then there will probably be one person playing lead and six people playing rhythm at the same time. That's a lot of rhythm. If every rhythm player would practice this theory, then it would be a lot easier on the lead player. Use your ears and be considerate of the person playing lead and the people who want to listen to the lead.*

- *When you are learning to flatpick, watch and listen to other flatpickers.*

- *Try to play with people who are better than you are.*

- *If you jam with guitarists who are not as good as you, don't "cut heads." This means you shouldn't try to play faster than everyone else can play. Don't smother lesser pickers with flash unless your intention is to intimidate them. The only time you want to play faster, hotter, and over their heads is when you are asked to. If you lie back, you will be asked back.*

- *Seek outlets for your music. In most cities you will find folk and bluegrass associations. Join the club. Go to the meetings and find out where all the jam sessions are.*

- *Take your time—don't rush progress. Have fun with your guitar.*

Discography

Norman Blake

County Records
Norman Blake and Red Rector CO-755

Flying Fish
The Fields of November FF-004
Old and New FF-010
Blackberry Blossom FF-047
Live at McCabes FF

Takoma
Directions

Rounder Records
Back Home in Sulpher Springs 0012
Whiskey Before Breakfast 0063
The Rising Fawn String Ensemble 0122
Full Moon on the Farm 0144
Original Underground Music from the Mysterious South 0166
Nashville Blues 0188
Light House on the Shore 0211
Nancy Blake's Grand Junction 0231
Norman Blake and Tony Rice Vol. 1 0233
Blind Dog 0254
Norman Blake and Tony Rice Vol. 2

Doc Watson

Flying Fish
Red Rockin' Chair FF-252
Doc and Merle Watson's Guitar Album FF-301
Pickin' the Blues FF-352

Quicksilver
Out in the Country QS-5031

(Doc Watson cont.)

Rounder Records
The Watson Family Tradition 0129
Down South SH-3742
Riding the Midnight Train SH-3752
Portrait SH-3759
On Praying Ground SH-3779
Doc Watson Sings Songs for Little Pickers SH-3786

Rutabaga
Favorites of Clint Howard and Doc Watson RR-3010

Vanguard
The Essential Doc Watson VMS-73108
The Essential Doc Watson Vol. 2 VMS-73121
Doc Watson on Stage VSD-009/10
Old Timey Concert VSD-107/8
Southbound VSD-79213

Tony Rice

Kaleidoscope
Acoustics F-010

Rebel
California Autumn REB-1549
Guitar REB-1582

Rounder Records
New Acoustic Music Sampler AN-02
Bluegrass 0092
Manzanita 0092
Mar West 0125
The Bluegrass Album Band 0140

(Tony Rice cont.)

Still Inside 0150
The Bluegrass Album Band Vol. 2 0164
Backwaters 0167
The Bluegrass Album Band Vol. 3 0180
Cold on the Shoulder 0183
Me and My Guitar 0201
The Bluegrass Album Band Vol. 4 0210
Native American 0248
The Bluegrass Album Band Vol. 5 0240
The Rice Brothers 0256

Sugar Hill
Church Street Blues SH-3732

Dan Crary

American Heritage
Bluegrass Guitar 275

Kicking Mule
Flatpicking Guitar KM-210

Rounder Records
Lady's Fancy 0099

Sugar Hill
Sweet Southern Girl SH-3707
Berline-Crary-Hickman SH-3720
Guitar SH-3730
Berline-Crary-Hickman SH-3739
B-C-H SH-3755
Take a Step Over SH-3770
And Now They Are Four SH-3773

Steve Kaufman

Thunderhead
Footloose with Red Rector

Kicking Mule
Flatpicking Guitars KM-210

Sleeping Bear Recordings
Frost on the Window 73185-00
Breaking Out 42090-01
Star of the County Down with Robin Kessinger
  72790-02
Strange Company with Nancy Brennan Strange,
  Don Cassell and Will Byers 90190-03
An Evening with Steve Kaufman video (VHS) with
  Will Byers 103090-04

Homespun Tapes
*Bluegrass Guitar Solos that Every Parking Lot
  Picker Should Know Vol. 1*

For a current listing and ordering information call
1-800-FLATPIK or 865-982-3808
E-mail to **Steve@FLATPIK.com**
Steve's World Wide Web Page Address is:
http://www.FLATPIK.com

or write to

**The Flatpicking Hotline
P.O. Box 1020
Alcoa, TN 37701**

Special thanks to:
Roy's Record Shop
Maryville, Tennessee
for helping with this discography